Spread A Little Sunshine

Edited by

Heather Killingray

First published in Great Britain in 1997 by
ANCHOR BOOKS
1-2 Wainman Road, Woodston,
Peterborough, PE2 7BU
Telephone (01733) 230761

HB ISBN 1 85930 545 8
SB ISBN 1 85930 540 7

Foreword

Anchor Books is a small press, established in 1992, with the aim of promoting readable poetry to as wide an audience as possible.

We hope to establish an outlet for writers of poetry who may have struggled to see their work in print.

The poems presented here have been selected from many entries. Editing proved to be a difficult task and as the Editor, the final selection was mine.

Spread A Little Sunshine is an inspiring collection of verse by people from all walks of life.

Each and every poem included within these pages portrays a number of different experiences which I am sure we can relate to.

So sit back, relax and enjoy this entertaining collection which you will be able to read time and time again.

I trust this selection will delight and please the authors and all those who enjoy reading poetry.

Heather Killingray
Editor

Contents

THE BIG SALE - A SORRY TALE!

Dear MPs, give us a better quality of life
If you cannot give a job to your honest loving wife
To sell all army homes to the Japanese
Tax payers and the public people are not pleased
Promises in the past all those lies!
Furious POWs all over Britain
Memories are back, all the pain
To sell to the Japs is a disgrace
It's a slap in the face
Wife's uncle killed by them in Singapore
Call a General Election let's have no more
Millions of pounds to all those fat cats
While homeless sleep in streets like rats!
Lottery cash NHS made better
All the truth is in this letter?

Scotch Tommy

BLIND BUT INDEPENDENT

I am blind
I am independent
It would be nice to see.
But it does not
stop me
from doing what you do.
I like playing games
I can still walk
and talk
I am blind
I am independent.

Lydia Jesson

JESUS WAS AN ALIEN

The star shone bright
That very night
But no-one really knew.
The way was clear
To bring him near
And from a babe he grew.

They trained him well
As all could tell
But no-one really knew.
He passed on love
From God above
So they could pass on too

He travelled wide
To be their guide
But no-one really knew.
He was so kind
He cured the blind
To live their lives anew.

'Twas time to leave
And all did grieve
But no-one really knew.
Was left at night
Alone to fight
And disappear from view.

Appeared again
To be a friend
But no-one really knew.
Lifted on high
Taken to the sky
He changed the earthly view.

Kathreen Hanson

Alien Hated

Jesus. Origins unknown -
Except the Bible's Truth
That says He came from Heaven's Throne
Before a babe, a youth!
Before an adult Jesus lived
And ruled with God on high
Until God sent Him as a gift -
Salvation to supply!
Time passed . . . and Mary bore her child,
Identified as Christ.
The Sinless Son, the Undefiled,
The Man that John baptised?!
The Holy Spirit led Him through
The crowds that He drew near . . .
Inspired souls that simply knew
God's Heavenly Child stood here!
Faith through Holy Revelation,
Belief in Him alone -
But prophecy decreed this nation
Would turn its heart to stone!
Thus Jesus, tortured to the end,
Died on a Cross of wood . . .
Crucified, as the Sinner's Friend,
Yet 'alien' . . . misunderstood . . .

Denis Martindale

The Easter Gospel Story

Spread the Easter Gospel Story,
When Christ, the Lord was crucified;
Our hopes, our dreams and our glory,
In Him, are surely magnified?
Hail to the Redeemer, Lord of light,
He shall redeem our souls tonight.

Spread the message far far afield,
Leap with wonder art the dear Lord;
Christ of the cross, our mighty Shield,
Proclaims the Father's Holy word.
Hail to the Redeemer, Lord of grace,
The Flame of God, reveals his face.

Spread the wonders of our great Christ,
Who rose from death's ephemeral phase,
A kingly soul so sacrificed;
He lives with us to endless days;
Hail to the Redeemer, Lord of faith,
Listen, children, to words He sayeth.

Spread the goodwill, yea, all around,
Like some Phoenix risen again,
Christ with wisdom and love profound,
Shall ride the storm and sprout the grain;
Hail to the Redeemer, Lord of life,
Blessing the lands with new harvests rife.

Spread the Easter Gospel Story,
Rejoice, rejoice - kneel down and pray;
The cross, the cross, . . . a victory,
For now Christ Jesus reigns for aye;
Hail to the Redeemer, Lord of all,
Supernal King on man shall call.

Grace Devina Priest

Jesus Was An Alien

Father Jesus thou hast told us the truth is out there
Open thine eyes heaven is all around, children be aware,
Bringer of light into a world so dark with despair,
Wonderful counsellor teach us how to love and how to care

Exalted above all others glorified brother and king,
Saviour to those without hope, your praises we sing,
Miracles granted in abundance, sweet parables thee bring,
Because thou hast gave up life, death has lost its sting,

Angels sing Holy Holy Lord God almighty Heaven's anthem
Behold, beauty purity, sits on the throne before them,
God's only son worshipped here on earth also heavenly cherubin,
Perfect Being, healer of the hard-hearted and sick amen,

Evidence surrounds us, splendid glories wonders and works,
Time space hath no boundaries, before thee lightning forks
Thunder rolls around Heaven when God talks to folks
Rays of hope in a gloomy world, where evil often stalks,

Jesus the Superstar shining brightly in Heaven's domain,
Soon Jesus will return again, but thy spirit did remain,
Holy spirit here amongst us, in our happiness and our pain
Next time our leader calls back here, won't leave us again,

So much talk of aliens, and circles in the corn,
But servants be careful, Satan's feeling so much scorn
He knows his days are numbered, so hurry become reborn,
If thou won't choose Jesus, instead a crown, given a thorn,

Folk say Jesus was an alien, the truth is out there,
Because he was so different, he gave his flesh to tear,
Father please forgive them, his enemies did hear,
He bore it well, for our sake, this how much he cares,

Such loving caring ways are supernatural to all of us,
Out of this world an alien, just believe what thou must.

Jordan

CHILD

(In memory to all who suffer
in body, mind and spirit)

The tears which I cry
To the pain I feel inside
When I'm not by your side
Just cast to one side
To being no-one's child.

> *My soul has been burdened*
> *To the coldness you left*
> *Deep within my heart*
> *My soul has been burdened*
> *To the numbness you left*
> *Deep within my heart.*

The tears which I feel
When thinking of the love
Love which I couldn't witness
I could only confess
This guilt and love to thee
To being no-one's child.

> *My soul has been burdened*
> *To the coldness you left*
> *Deep within my heart*
> *My soul has been burdened*
> *To the numbness you left*
> *Deep within my heart.*

The tears I need to express
To the bitterness which has strayed
And stayed around far too long
So bless my soul to bow
In walking forth to your love and grace
To becoming someone's child.

My soul has been burdened
To the coldness you left
Deep within my heart
My soul has been burdened
To the numbness you left
Deep within my heart.

Now these tears have been cleansed
Let my soul witness to touch
With your love and compassion
For now I can appreciate and see
In those souls which aren't free
To being no-one's child.

My soul has been burdened
To the coldness you left
Deep within my heart
My soul has been burdened
To the numbness you left
Deep within my heart.

M A Twidale

KEEP FIT

Caught sight of my reflection just the other day
When I saw the bulges, thought wonder what I weigh?
Feeling apprehensive I stood upon the scales
As I watched the needle spin, I really went quite pale.
Been on lots of diets never saw them through
Better join the Keep Fit, yes that's the thing to do.

Yvonne King

UNTITLED

Cash, can this a currency
Divide the rich and poor,
Life, this life, it's all free
Is anything worth more

No sum existence could produce
Beauty, nature have no price
Eternal, nothing can decide
Its value or its size

No man has right enough to make
An empire worth more
No President, no head of state
Can change it by his laws

True wealth dealt equally to all
To share and share alike
All creatures be they large or small
Have this their single right

Money? Just a grain of sand
Turned and churned by nature's tide
True wealth is spread by nature's hand
And equally to all supplied

Can gold and silver take the place
Of air we breathe or soil we tread
Can tokens of this earthly life
Buy that life of nature bred

Are coloured bank notes more required
Than spring's new growth or autumn's hue
Are more man's printed sheets required
Than nature's payments, to all due.

Graham Charles Brabbins (Deceased)

Our Own Personal Angel

(To Merna's dearly departed Mother, and Michael's dearly departed Grandmother, with all our most genuine eternal love and effection. For Marjorie, you must surely be our own personal angel.)

Our Own Personal Angel was always there when we needed her.
Our dearly departed Marjorie would genuinely have both
The time and the patience to hear us.
With her truly kindly worlds,
And her very lovely deeds,
She constantly shone as an amazingly powerful beacon
In a dark world filled with ceaseless despair.

No sincerely delightful soul such as her
Should ever have endured the most painfully horrible afflictions imaginable.

Now our still greatly cherished loved one is
Peacefully thriving within our Heavenly Father's Real Paradise
Such is where there is only permanently bountiful contentment to be found.

Dearest, we certainly wish you well,
As we will indeed confidently see you again,
Never more to be parted from one another -
For you must surely be our Own Personal Angel.

Michael Merna

My Children

Children of mine I say to you
My heart is full of love
Children of mine I say to you
My life is yours for ever
Did you know children of mine
I was born to be your Mother.

Caroline Nash

Very Special Mum

Now, a very special mum,
is that certain someone,
And secrets you can share,
because a mum will always care.

She's always on your side,
no matter what you hide.
And support she will give,
which we all need as we live.

The love you share, that has no cost
is truly a love, never lost,
She'll always be there with a kiss
even when life is just hit and miss.

When you break down and cry
your mum will never pry.
When you have made that terrible mistake,
your mum is there to give you a break.

No, you don't have to explain,
all the heartache and pain,
Why? Because that certain someone,
is my very special mum.

S Simpson

Lights Out

When tragedy strikes, and the future's blue
You know in your heart that it's over
And that it's lights out for you
You lay down and look at the ceiling
Nothing much more you can do
Things cannot change for the better
It has to be lights out for you

Your life flashes past in memories
Not again will the sun shine through
The final curtain is waiting
It's surely lights out for you
The good times are what you remember
The people so loving and true
A shadow comes over the ceiling
Because the lights have gone out for you.

Dee Husay

LOOKING BACK

As we sit in the hammock at dusk
Remembering the person we have lost,
One year ago today.

We watch the night clouds arrive
To form pictures and scenes in our minds,
Like one year ago today.

I remember the style of the sun as it set
And the clouds across the rising moon,
July, one year ago today.

It really was an eerie night sky,
The colours bright and yet disturbing
To us, one year ago today.

We have thought about that time,
Thoughts both painful and yet kind,
About one year ago today.

Tears still invade, tumbling down our cheeks,
Remembering we had to say goodbye.
One year ago today.

A E Broughton

THOUGHTS OF MUM AND DAD

'Tis now ten years to the day,
Since my dear mother passed away.
She lies now 'neath that depth of soil;
No more can she a kettle boil.

She used to love her cup of tea,
With bread and jam she shared with me.
That was all mum could afford,
But for it she always thanked the Lord.

My poor dad was killed in the war;
A dear man who I never saw.
A photo of him is all I see;
In place of pride it will always be.

He was the bravest man of all,
So people say who can recall.
No fight would he let others share;
He was just brave beyond compare.

That day when someone took his life,
They also 'killed' his darling wife,
For though she lived on, it must be said,
Mum had often wished that she was dead.

Well now she lies down there below,
A nicer mum one could not know.
So now I kneel and lay a wreath,
And say a prayer for mum beneath.

I rise again now to my feet,
With thoughts of dad I did not meet;
So thinking of them both today,
I shed some tears and walk away.

Fred Neville

To My Daughter Getting Married

Is this my child I bore long ago?
Is this my child I loved to watch grow?
Is this my child to whom I gave life?
Is this my child soon to become a wife?

I remember the school-days, the friends that you had
Sitting in our kitchen, yes, sometimes I got mad!
But mainly we had fun, they were a super crowd
Even though occasionally they were certainly very loud!

Your gym days were memorable, a very talented girl,
The back-flicks, somersaults, you were always in a whirl,
But after that, we then moved on to something I loved, horses,
Rosie (favourite), Peaches, Cointreau, didn't we walk some courses?

And then of course the time came for you to move away
But I never thought you would actually choose to live in the USA
But Bill came along and you were hooked, almost from day one
And then like magic, the next part of your life had just begun

After we had been to stay, we both thought Bill was charming,
So now the thought of you getting married isn't quite so alarming,
Of course with you being so far away, that will *always* hurt
But we will sneak up on you for a holiday, so always be on the alert!

Well darling, we wish you love, happiness and laughter
And of course that you will be 'Happy ever after'
Just remember that no matter how many miles we're apart
You will always be uppermost and closest in our hearts.

Also, should you need us at any time at all
You know to just pick up the phone and give us a quick call,
And if it is within our power you know we'll do it with pleasure
So please keep sending letters, photos, everything we can treasure.

Hazel Markham

A Mother's Love

When times are hard and you're feeling low,
When you've lost a friend and it's a bitter blow,
Remember I'm here and I'm feeling your pain
And that all of life is a long winding lane,
Around every corner there is something to gain.
And it's that little something which compensates pain,
If you concentrate hard you will feel my embrace,
And the gentle pressure of my kiss on your face,
Whatever you suffer and wherever you go,
Whatever you feel I want you to know
That I am beside you and giving you strength
Whatever the reason whatever the length
I know you can't touch me or my face even see
But my love is so strong it will reach you, you'll see,
I will give you the strength to get over this loss
Because I'm your mum and you know I'm the boss.

Jean Gentili

The Big Black Cat

What's that in the garden
Watching a bird?
I call to him softly
But I don't think he heard,
'Tis a big black cat.

I call him once more,
Louder I call,
He pricks up his ears
But that is all,
The big black cat.

A dog gives a bark,
The bird flies away
High into the sky,
He's safe for today
From the big black cat.

Marian Smith

Near Death To Rest In Peace

As I sat and stared in wonder and amazement,
It was as if it wanted to touch me, to hurt me,
I froze as it stared back with those ice-cold eyes,
Why me? I whimpered, why me?

I can't explain the fear I felt,
So cold, so numb, entranced,
It spoke to me,
I stared in awe,
I knew I had to get away, get out!

It came close to me with arms astride,
Its ice-cold fingers flicked through my hair,
Then around my neck I felt its hands,
Gripping as if to hurt me, to kill me.

For a second I lost consciousness,
As the breath was squeezed from my body,
Then after a last attempt to kill me,
I managed to grasp a breath of air, of life.

Then I awoke to see this apparition slowly fading,
With a smile on its face, as if to say,
'I've done what I had to, to be
Laid to rest, to rest in peace.'

Linsay Galloway

SHE

She was sat there reading a book
When the bumps began upstairs,
The lights began to dim
Her pupils really flared.

It was the same nearly every night
When the clock was chiming ten,
Things began to happen
Driving her round the bend.

She'd only moved in last week
To a cottage many years old,
With a long haunting history,
Thirty years it had took to be sold.

She cared nothing for ghosts or spooks
A believer she never had been,
But now she began to wonder
About things she thought she'd seen.

Her skin began to creep
A chill was in the air,
The shadow came from nowhere
Hovering behind her chair.

She froze within her seat
And decided then and there
That maybe she should have listened
But it was too late, for her to care.

Her heart had stopped already
When her husband stroked her hair,
'Did I make you jump sweetheart?
I've mended the fuse upstairs!'

G J Chadwick

FAX ME A LAGER

'Lager, lager, lager,'
Bought on a CD,
Stacked alongside CD computer games,
To be played when it rains,
Then it's on with the TV,
To see what you can see,
Sat eating your microwave dinner,
Interrupted with your cordless telephone,
Somebody wanting a fax sent around the world,
Then out into your car,
Be it Metro or be it Jaguar,
You're expected to have one whoever you are,
Past the supermarket and DIY,
To park in the mall with everything to buy,
Shop, book a holiday,
Pay the bills you have to pay,
And all under the one roof,
All in the same place,
Still time to watch football,
As into your car you race,
Watch the match then back home for tea,
Then get ready to go out for a dance,
Doubtless in one of the clubs you'll find romance,
And whilst you're out 'Lager, lager, lager' you shout,
As the music blares out,
The fighting lads, the waiting girls,
The courting ritual, the mating game,
Which no matter which century stays the same,
As things change with new technologies,
Life as it is in the 1990's.

Paul Waldock

Dead?

How long have I lain here? I really can't say.
It could be a week. Or just maybe a day
My doctor I heard saying I'd died
Of nothing suspicious it was suicide
He certified that I was dead
So why do I lie here full of sorrow and dread?
I can't see above me and I can't see below
Am I dead of alive? I really don't know
I've lain here and wondered is death just a lie
Do I stay here forever and curl up and cry?
Are there other bodies beside me - under the ground
Listening and waiting just to be found
And if we're found I wonder by whom.
Who could really come knocking on the
lid of my tomb
An angel who'd take me to St Michael's gold gates?
Or a devil who'll take me to someone who hates.
But something is coming and it's coming here.
I've heard a slight tapping which fills me with fear.
Now I don't care if I'm alive or I'm dead
As long as something is coming to end this great dread

James Joseph McKenna

Dux Fidelis

The ducks upon the Dodder River
Greet with quacks the breadcrumb giver,
Until the gulls in wintertime
Grab their bread before they dine.

But those mean gulls, in search of self,
In the summertime go north;
The ducks have waited patiently
And now their young are coming forth.

We, like those ducks, must persevere
When the winter seems severe.
In our time of greatest need
Our God will turn out true indeed.

Michael Thompson

PUMPKIN

An orange glow,
A yellow grin,
Flickering candle,
Golden chin,

Vivid shine,
Stunning power,
Round and evil,
The witching hour,

Brilliant shades,
Gaudy reds,
Intensely glowing,
Pumpkin heads,

Vibrant sections,
Radiant stare,
Amber pulp,
Beware, beware,

Enchanted feelings,
Bright and clear,
A face of nightmares
A face to *fear!*

Natasha Wielogorska (11)

The Capricious Shoemaker

Thirty years ago he mended shoes:
'Cobbler, cobbler, mind my shoe
Get it done by half past two.'

Now he drives a car, a Jaguar:
'Half past two is much too soon,
Get it done by afternoon.'

Once so poor he worked by candlelight
on rubber soles and leather soles,
peep toes and square toes,
tapping into sling backs
and nailing clod-hoppers and high heels.

While on the last went buckle shoes,
winklepickers, beetlecrushers,
slip-ons and lace-ups
as he slaved and burned the midnight oil.

Some thought he was an elvin shoemaker,
'Afternoon is much too late,
Get it done by half past eight.'

Hoarding up his gold for thirty years
while his wife and family
thin and wan, looked on.

He had no use for wise philosophy
when he went and bought his Jag.
He stuffed his boot with brand new shoes
and kept his brothel-creepers in a bag.

Sheila Bath

SPRINGTIME

Flowers bloom, bees hum and birds sing
Around the garden in late spring
Hedges trimmed and borders weeded
Bare lawn patches newly seeded.

Don't worry about how it was
It is upsetting and your loss
Heavy falls of rain and snow
Dulls the mind and makes one slow.

Damage can be done by frost
Blackened leaves and seedlings lost
Stamping on the hardened ground
Wishing for the spring-like sounds

Open up the lockered shed
Oh those tools feel like lead
Aching back and tired muscles
Disturb the ants and make them bustle.

Insects of all kinds and stages
Have been lying hidden there for ages
Made active by the warming sun
Finding work and damage to be done.

Standing back and looking on
With winter debris almost gone
Fresh shoots and leaves and buds
Springing up from leaves and mud.

Spring is such a lovely time
When crickets sing and bluebells chime
The sun just warm enough to please
And fledglings fly on scented breeze.

J Funnell

The Daffodil

We've all had them in our gardens, you and I.
Heads held high, stretching tall to the sky
Displayed in our gardens, making them bright
Filling our hearts with sheer delight.
After the dark miserable, winter days,
Our planting and waiting finally pays
Lanky and tall, their stems all green
Their golden heads a sight to be seen
Now the time has come, the flowers are done
They've finished their glory in the warm spring sun
Drooping heads, now looking quite sad
Such a wonderful show we've all just had
Now petals and trumpets are all crumpled and torn
Their leaves all sagging, shredded and worn
See those leaves as they begin to die down
As the goodness seeps back into their weary crown
Now jobs all done, it's time to rest
So when spring reappears, they'll be at their best
We'll all patiently wait until
You re-appear our Golden Daffodil.

Yvonne Monks

Gale Winds

I stood by the window looking out,
I watched the wind lashing about,
Knocking down fences, breaking down trees,
Wrecking everything just as it pleased.

Paper and bags flying about,
Making small children, scream and shout,
Swirling leaves into the sky,
Making it hard for the birds to fly.

Howling down chimneys, whistling through gaps
Making old men hold onto their caps.
Knocking down bird tables onto the ground,
Blowing around everything that it found.

Taking the breath from the people it meets,
Pushing and pulling them off of their feet.
Whipping cars and lorries from off of the road
Causing destruction wherever it goes.

Denise Jeffcoate

WINTER WINDS

As winter winds sweep down o'er mountain tops and hills,
And snowflakes fall upon the rocky crags
And from this lofty perch I sometimes see a watery sun arising
Then clouds rise higher in the springtime sky
Stags will look for mates in warming climes
And sky will fill with birds, descending on my rocky home
Breezes bring the smell of blossom from the world below,
Then summer days are long and sweet
But now I see the days were short when once
I wooed my love upon this very spot,
'Twas then I found she did not want my love, but he
He who was a finer friend, I thought
Did strike behind and brought
The misery, sorrow, grief that come
With losing one as lovely as the summer sun.
I took his life that day, amidst the rocks that made his bed.
My penance then was sure, to walk these hills for evermore,
And haunt this place of strife, that made and took my life.

Len Adams

The New Witch

The new witch
Nervously
Ties L-plates
To a brand new broomstick
Ready for the first
Midnight ride.
Pricks her finger,
Missing the wax effigy
And mixes
Eye of newt
With Cuppa Soup
In a cauldron
Bought
From the Co-op.

Paul Wilkins

Hot Summer's Day

To be content, on a summer's day
To lie in the warmth, and drift away
Remembering the good times and the bad
On a day like today, no-one should be sad
Lying here looking at a clear blue sky
The sweet smell of flowers floating by
The birds are singing, they're happy today
Memories of cold winters, fading away
Children are playing, having fun
Under the glow of a summer's day sun
To lie and relax, and just feel good
On a hot summer's day, everyone should.

Kathy Iley

RAIN

Rain is falling to the ground,
Silently without a sound,
Pitter, patter, on it goes,
Soaks my head, and wets my toes.
I go to bed,
It must be said,
The rain goes on all night,
In the morning still the rain,
Pitter, patters on the pane
Oh what a boring sight!
A glimpse of sun,
The rain goes on,
I long for fun,
It can't be long.
I can't believe my eyes,
The rain has gone away
I can get some exercise
I can go out and play,

The rain has gone
Chased by the sun,
My interest now,
Is far more fun.
A beautiful rainbow in the sky,
The biggest ever to catch my eye.
It has its beginning in the sea
And seems to end right here by me!

Kayleigh Alexandre (10)

NOVEMBER SUN (FALSE IMPRESSIONS)

White, wintry sun, why do you shine?
Deceiving the world that everything's fine.
Smiling so coldly on those down below,
Hiding the truth of things that you know.
White, seemingly harmless, passing clouds float,
While, in your heavens, so cruelly you gloat.
What show are you planning to spring on our days?
Pretending to warm us with deceptive bright rays.
Here, where it's winter, you emulate spring
With cold, bright blue heavens where winter birds sing.
The naked earth's beauty displayed in your light,
So peacefully fooled into forgetting their plight,
Losing resistance, lulled by the day,
Calmed into contentment for which they will pay.
I see behind it, that false look of cheer,
The warning of peril I continually hear.
My outward appearance emulates yours,
While inside I'm crying and heartbreak endures.
That's how I know you, your brightness is mine,
Telling the world that everything's fine.
I know your game - I constantly play -
False face, a smile and bluffing my way!

Wendy P Frost

SPRING SONNET

Bridlepath, bordering Hesketh's high field
Where rape grown grossly blonde
Bestows disinfectant fragrance on the world,
Direct and simple, runs to wicketed bluebell wood;

And half-way, a steel gate oversees long northern path
- Strauss's eternal green descending final theme -
Cascading mile on heavenly mile to far village clump.
At this junction, a small outcome in another direction:

Khaki-smart, a lone pheasant's egg rests uncapped on the dirt,
Its glossy milk-white inside void, except a saffron splash
Left by magpie or stoat to harden in its tiny pool.

Above, cloud-strewn sky, sunny, fresh and clear,
Below, clods burst with weed on vacant track,
Between, cracked shell, empty of all but air.

A Cohen

Fun With A Cold Nose

I want to be a dog
Cute and furry a black one
I wouldn't pull when we walked
I wouldn't mind when you talked
I'd always be pleased to see you
In any state of mind
I'd lick you all over
In heaven in clover
I'd sit on your lap
roll on my back
waver my paw
beg for more
I'd jump on your bed
rub my cold nose
I'd have such fun
until you rose
but I'd whine
when you left me
I'd chew up your shoe
not naughty - nothing else to do.

Linda D Shropshire

AARON JOHN

(On the occasion of the birth of our first grandchild, born on our wedding anniversary)

This week was our thirtieth anniversary,
We all waited with bated breath in the nursery,
And then it happened! - 'Twas over and done,
To John and Jaan, a wonderful son,
So, John's a proud father, and the mother is Jaan,
Robert's a Grandad and Cathie's a Gran,
When they first let us see him, that wonderful night,
The vote was unanimous, - it was love at first sight.

For Aaron John was a sight to behold,
As he shouted a welcome, in tones loud and bold,
As we gazed down in wonder at this little man,
We gave thanks, for the touch of the Dear Master's hand.
He has given Jaan the strength, for this wonderful night.
And he gave us all Aaron, - 'The Giver of Light'.

Robert French

SUMMER DREAMS

Winds of change, move swiftly in Summer Dreams.
Our lives, a jigsaw of photographic images.
Some in sepia print -
intertwine and then move on,
to capture future pages,
a storyboard of days.
- a collection of life's visions.
Misty edged pictures, cling to rose coloured canvas.
Our Winter eyes turn to Summer hopes,
changing times - changing lives.

Annette Jones

Photography

Trees stripped of their leaves
and photographed against a cloudy sky,
make superb silhouettes
like fairies dancing by.

Look for individual trees
or clumps uncluttered and striking,
familiar and unusual things
whatever's to your liking.

Bridges, chimneys, gates and a steeple
streams, and waterfalls, maybe people,
a glowing sunset or stormy sky
or a wood pigeon flying high.

A winter bonus for photographers
is early frost and mist,
a spider's web covered in dew
should be on your list.

Pine cone hanging from a branch
or a fountain in a park
pale watery winter sunlight
or bats flying in the dark.

So go for a brisk walk
get a glow in your cheeks,
take four rolls of film
and shoot pictures for weeks.

Y P Bacon

Rainforest

If you go down to the woods today
you're in for a big surprise,
if you go down to the woods today
you'll never believe your eyes.
For ev'ry tree that ever there was
is crashing down for certain because,
today's the day
the woodcutters have their business.

Picnic time for animals,
are the animals
having a lovely time today
behind steel bars and unaware
the wipe-out of their habitat?
Too few glades and water pools,
its concrete floors
and lots of prying eyes.
At six o'clock
their mummies and daddies
can't take them home to bed,
because their homes are not in the zoo.

Chris Antcliff

It Isn't Fair

Dear Lord, it isn't fair -
        Here I am at eighty-four
And younger men have gone before.
        (Really, I am eighty-seven)
They have beat me into heaven!

Dear Lord, it isn't kind -
        George is deaf and Sam is blind,
But I can hear a thrush's song
        And see the daisies. It seems wrong.

I cannot understand your ways.
Some have drab and lonely days,
But mine are filled with memories dear,
The mail brings letters of good cheer!

Dear Lord, I cannot understand,
But thank you for your loving hand.
What have I done to win all this?
And on my cheek a grandchild's kiss!

John Urwin

Can I Help You?

'A secretary - how interesting' was what I often heard
When I worked at the infirmary, the heart of city hard,
Each day I went and never knew just what would happen, when,
But uncertainty is stimulating, at hospital, life began!

The patients were around each day, some quiet, some disturbed,
My job was just to help, a smile, and a pleasant word,
And it gave great satisfaction, although they all were ill
I could at least try hard and make their visit not so dull.

I typed and wrote, took notes and talked, saw doctors by the score,
And met the nurses, cleaners, staff, each day till half past four,
I learned a different language, oesophagus, otitis, gall,
Each patient has a working part with need of overhaul.

Some days were trying, long and hard, with more work than before,
But there was always something happening in theatre, ward or floor,
To make me think and thank our God for health body all,
For these poor folks were needing help, it's free and there for all.

So don't let's knock the NHS, it's improving all the while,
But thank the staff who try to help by giving them a smile!

Elizabeth M Sudder

THE FISHERMAN'S DAUGHTER

There are times when I am good
Or I've done something well at school,
Or I've had my hair cut short
And I need telling it looks cool!
Or my bicycle needs mending,
That's when I can't help wishing
I had an ordinary dad,
Instead of one 'gone fishing!'.

But at times I'm not so clever.
Like the times I've made Mum mad,
And she's been shouting all day long -
'Just wait 'til I tell your Dad!'
Then it's an early night for me,
My Daddy's darling daughter -
I hope and pray he'll stay quite late,
Fly fishing by the water.

But you know, soon, when I'm grown up,
(To my mother's great concern!)
The noble art of fly fishing
Is what I intend to learn.
And when Dad's taught me all he knows
I really will be glad,
For then I'll leave a note for Mum
'Gone fishing - with my Dad!'

G Alexandre

SUNSET

The immortal orb begins to slip slowly from the sky,
Drawn by an invisible force towards the knife-edged horizon.
Silhouetted trees are woven into an intricate pattern of branches
and leaves;
Like ebony statues they stand proudly against a myriad of burnished
hues,
Abstractly arranged in fading streaks and subtly blended with gold
tinged clouds.
Bird song is absorbed into the quiet ambience and a respectful silence
falls
As life's radiant ruler transforms incandescence into a dusky black
blanket,
That softly envelopes all life and customarily ends another day.

Zahra Lalani

THE SEEDS OF LOVE

Those eyes of blue that hypnotise
A heart that's of pure gold
They both hold many secrets
Of mysteries untold
You're the one that fills my daydreams
That makes my sun beam bright
When faraway, I miss you
Without you, life is night
Tall and dark - but handsome?
Perhaps to mine eyes alone
A faithful trust from nothing
The seeds of love were sown

There let them flourish, let it show
That from blooms of love, flowers may grow.

S J Robinson

STRANGER

Rushing home; can't be late
Not yet dark.
'Quick hurry up' my sister calls
'Mum will be waiting, we'll be done for sure!'
Running and panting; must get home
'Stop! Wait a minute' I call
'I've something in my shoe.'
We stop and rest to sort it out;
It's really quiet, no-one about.
'Sssh, did you hear that?' my sister asked.
I listened and slowly turned my head
My heart began to beat so fast.
This scruffy man so mean and rough
Just staring right at both of us.
He smiled and beckoned with his hand
'Come with me' he seemed to say
Should we go or should we stay?
He started to walk towards us
I now sense some fear
We both turn and start to run
'Oh why can't mum be here?'
Keep on running; don't look behind
Home is just ahead.
Running up the garden path, knocking on the door
Calling out for mum to come.
Safe at last in our beds frightened no more
We shan't be going over there anymore!

Adam Johnson (12)

British Pastimes

The British have a variety of sports and hobbies, love football
in the winter season
Tennis is a summer sport, and Wimbledon draws the crowds,
with the favourite winner in mind, for a reason.
Boat racing Cambridge and Oxford, the crowds shout when the
oars are rowing at a great pace
This is a great challenge for a river sport to have a great race.
Some enjoy horse racing and the thrill of placing a bet,
to hopefully win
The crowds jump up and down and wave their hands, and make
such a din.
Photography is a favourite hobby, and enthusiasts like to snap
a colourful nature scene
Then show to friends, for a remembrance of a lifelong dream.
Bird-watching in the woods early in the morning
And hear different songbirds when day is dawning.
I have several hobbies, which are relaxing, and bring me peace of
mind and a day long joy which is so serene
A walk in the park, ducks swimming along the gentle winding stream.
I see flowers blooming, children playing, each one having
so much fun
The sun glistening through the treetops, and fading when day is done.
I have a great imagination, and so writing poetry takes me
to another world which is full of great pleasure
This enables me to relax, and I am free of stress, and this is my leisure
I walk by the ocean, and I see sailboats with coloured sails,
and hear rustling and blowing
This is a wondrous sight, and I imagine great ventures, of where
they are all going.

Joyce Willis

When I Was Five And You Were Ten

Why can't life be easy like way back then when I was five
and you were ten?
I arrived a few weeks early. They said 'Oh dear I think she's dead.'
And put me in a box under the bed. Then they took another look
and found me breathing - 'Let's christen her quick as she won't last.'
'What shall we call her? Norma - Oh that's nice.'
Why can't life be easy?
I started school with my best friend. We learnt to read and to do our
sums in parrot fashion - that was the rule way back then . . .
We went to junior school as we grew up, we'd country dance, we'd
giggle and laugh, then Mrs Goy would say 'Get in the corner
until you stop.'
The old tin bath came out on Friday nights - the clothes horse round.
The towels hung the fire alight - sparks flying out as you
took your turn.
We went to toilet by torch or candlelight and used old
newspapers hung in squares upon the door. Then the shit cart came
and took it away to the farmer's field at the end of the lane.
Why can't life be easy?
I was sick and I was ill rolling about in agony. Eventually the doctor
came and then she said 'How are you? You've got a temperature
you've got flu' as I rolled out of bed half dead. I used to scream
and then I'd shout.
You smacked my legs and sent me out. I loved you then -
I love you now.
Why can't life be easy like way back then when I was five
and you were ten?

Why?

Norma Spillett

HOTSHOTS

Back in the eighties Steve was champ - a cut above the rest
The Nugget bore the Davis stamp - to be the very best

World number two who found renown - in such a classy style
Was Tony Knowles from Bolton Town - *The Melter* with the smile

The Whirlwind Jimmy had the nerve to make the boldest move
So fascinating to observe when he was in the groove

Cliff talked in a Canadian drawl, and once he wore the crown
The Grinder's pace was like a crawl - he wore his victims down

Then Alex from the Emerald Isle would twitch, and then he blew
The Hurricane - a hundred mile an hour went charging through

Count Dracula - he played his part - Ray Reardon in disguise
A practised master of his art - before our very eyes.

They could be actors in a scene - for they could call the shots
A battle on a field of green - with kisses plants and pots

With cushions for the high-breaks too, and pockets - sometimes tight
Balls - yellow, brown and green and blue - a black, a pink, a white

Some chalk, a triangle of reds - a coin is tossed to choose
A white-gloved referee calls 'Heads' - the players take their cues

One strikes then he is on a run - a whisper of delight
The enrapt audience thinks a one-four-seven's on tonight!

New faces join the hallowed ranks - now famous as the rest
But I would like to offer thanks to six of snooker's best!

Arlene Skerratt

Unscrambled Scrabble

All our families love to dabble
With a challenging game of Scrabble.
Pick your letters, then make a word,
Of which they say, they've never heard.
With our dictionaries on first hand,
The game is going well to plan.
Up to seven-letter words we make,
Extra fifty points on the break.
Spelling, scheming all the time,
Around the board or all in line.
Helps your minds to unfold,
Relaxation for the young and old.

Pat Garvey

The Home Coming

As I walk up the path
And knock on the door
Thoughts go back years,
To when I walked from that door
A few hasty words
I thought I knew best
But the years have gone swiftly
I'm no longer a lad
Growing up has not been all fun.
Then the front door is open'd
An old man stands there
He stares for a moment
'Welcome home son.'

M Parnell

FT

Climb your tree and take a look,
What you see, could make a book.
Not the tree with bright green leaves,
The tree of life and what it means.
The best hobby I've found in years,
Is searching for my long lost heirs.
Ancestors in their far back days,
Perhaps like you in many ways.
Farmers mostly, who tilled the land,
Does gardening easily come to hand?
No transport and nowhere to go,
Only their valley did they know.
If you want to make new friends,
Climb your tree it never ends.
Places on maps not known before,
Look closer you'll see a lot more.
Searching for family far and wide,
Oh! What a thrill, when one you find.
American cousins you find, what glee
Which branch on your tree could they be?
Oh yes! It's grandad's sister-in-law,
Your grandad, brothers, he had four.
Across to Canada where one went,
It's said this one was quite a gent.
Your family's spread far and wide,
It's just great fun to search and find.
What a shame they're not alive,
But what a shock if they did arrive.
Some think this hobby is dry and dull,
The opposite I find, it's full of fun.
Don't believe me! Try it yourself,
An addict you'll be, you'll find at length
This hobby you've got for years to come,
Then you're gone, and the search starts for you.

Geraldine Ward

THE DREAM HOBBY

My hobby is watching the TV
As I sit on this chair so comfortably
Stuffing my snacks down and drinking my tea
Oh what a joy this brings to me
Because as I've grown old and am very shaky
The TV brings the world to me to see
As I sit in this dormitory
I can still remember the times I was active
Playing football, and rugby for my clubs and my country
Now all I can do is go to the pub and recall
the times when I was young
Oh well as I go back to watch my TV
In my chair that's so comfy dipping my
biscuits in my tea
Now all I can do is support my favourites
on the TV
And hope they can win for me
As I have a little bet hopefully I'll have
A nice little bundle coming to me
Oh what a joy my hobby brings to me
As I watch my TV and drink my tea
So goodnight and God bless me and my TV.

Mark Thorpe

SELF-BEAUTY

I'm fat, black and ugly, but do I care? No!
I'm what I am, and that's all that matters,
I target vitality and not the pre-planned,
Sorry about the illusions this shatters.

If my voice doesn't echo sophistication,
I recommend you attend to what I'm saying,
This isn't some actress perfecting a script,
And this is not some vast part that I'm playing.

If you want a performance, you'll have to take me,
I'll do no transforming for you,
The significance I have is entirely in me,
And I'm not about to give it another hue.

D Wade

SPORT

Played for Beds County hockey
And it was also to be
A wonderful year for me
As you will very soon see.

For County tennis, I, too
Managed without a to-do.
Enjoyed them both very much
And wouldn't you, my old Dutch!

Not much longer after this
My golf handicap now is
Quite a low number of *eight*
It's never, never too late.

Work at your sport when you can
Try always to beat a man
Then you know you will be good
And it will be understood.

As you have always done well
Everyone able to tell
You do not wish any more
Have certainly gained full score.

Gwendoline Albon

Encounter On Skye

(To Candice)

A kerosene blast across a shrouded dawn,
A concrete timpani of sound.
A small man rode the fruits of science
Beyond the pull of ground.
A smaller man, upon a Cuillin crag
Sat waiting for the sun, to make the day,
To warm the way, to make the summit fun.
The pilot in the cockpit tight,
Observed the Cuillin's tower.
Then at mach one, from a new-born sun,
Turned on the awesome power.
The climber sat, Mars bar in hand,
From across the Sound of Sleat,
He saw the plane, its gleaming frame,
Its after-burning heat.
Two thousand feet, the pilot banked,
Along the black escarpment,
Two thousand five, the climber turned
To wonder in amazement.
Below him there, in calm sea air
The aviation master, like him, the plane
It too could climb, but just a little faster!
The climber and the flyer
Acknowledged one another, in swift respect,
And some regret, they called each other 'brother',
Then as the pilot pulled away,
The climber, he just sat,
Both parting with the mutual thought,
'Wish I were doing that!'

Edwin W Tomkins

To See Your Face

Amid tumultuous turbulence, of darkness and light,
Millions, struggled in the fight, for life.
I performed the deeds, at tremendous speeds
Millions of tiny pulsating lights fell, into darkness.
Surrounded by countless warriors I fought
And when it seemed I would come to nought
I do not know how, I do not know why.
With a final shout, I was out! First. Alone in a place.
Within a soft embrace.
There, there was no strife
But I was full of life
Feeding through my navel,
In a watery cradle.
Secure and content, just as was meant.
Before this I knew, a chance to be with you.

The trials and tribulations I bore
Now at birth will there be more?
Please show me this place
I have travelled for eons to see your face.
I wonder, what's the meaning?
As I hear myself screaming!
Is this an omen, a sign?
For the inheritance to be mine?
After the strain, the worry, the pain.

I feel your eyes, your relief, your smile.
Your adoring face my prize
Your joy and love without lies
Your comforting arms where I lie
I hear myself coo. So happy to be with you.
I am! Your child.

Reynold Henry Duncan

The Mistress

The mistress swoops upon her game
Like a bird of prey on a mammal lame
She vultures and devours all she can prey
Her selfish hunger makes her day

She kisses and canoodles with her weakened capture
And relishes in her own rapture
Her heart lies false unto all around
Still she continues the treatment so neat - so profound

Her head held high way in the sky
While watching the hurt making others die
The tidal wave that she's created
Affects so many and floods out hatred

Her joyous conceit her plan so neat
Brings the wife begging at her feet
'Please stop the pain the tortuous torment
For me my husband for me he was meant
You captured him while we were vulnerable
And temptation's resistance was uncontrollable
Unable to fight the hardships we muster
When a marriage falls flat
And bad times do cluster'

Yet the ever-toiling wife remains in her loyal duty
Enduring the pains
Pain of watching family and friends offering their hearts
For they too feel the same

And while the mistress walks out with her man
The bitterness twists and kills all that it can
Like a whirlwind it's bellowed through mother and child
Through brother and sister driving them wild
Wild with the pain that they must endeavour
As the mistress runs free - forever and ever.

Lorraine Gould

My Mother

My
mother
is
the
best
in
the
world
she
is
tremendous
in fact
she's
the
greatest
I
can
hardly
explain
her

Kim Lennon (7)

Daffodils Revisited

I wandered lonely as a cloud,
And saw, beneath the trees,

Daffodils, bright miser's gold,
Earth hoard, parting the soil.

The end of a cold winter.

Stan Downing

HEARTACHE

I don't want you to call me Mummy
I don't want you to come and stay
I don't want you to give me love
I want you to accept me some day.
I know I have no claim to you
Especially after all this time
I might not have looked after you
But I still feel you are mine.
I couldn't afford to keep you
I couldn't just end it either
I couldn't live with the guilt
So I ended up doing neither.
There was only one other option
And that was to give you away
Even though I couldn't manage
I wanted to make someone's day.
Every year I remember you
Especially on your birthday
I sometimes think of meeting you
Trying to think what I'd say.
I don't want you to live with me
I just want to see your face
I need to know who you are
To fill this empty space.

V Weekes

MY LOVELY MOTHER

I really love my Mother
She is like no other
From my delight to despair
My Mother is always there.

Douglas J Hazard

WHOSE WAY IS BEST?

Many things throughout the day no notice need at all.
Done that way so frequently, reason just can't recall.
Suddenly a neighbour says to you right out of blue,
'Why do that job differently from how all others do?'
You stare for a long moment, she's given you a shock.
You've never thought about it, you've done it such a lot.
She makes you feel quite angry so you firmly say,
'It's way I've always done it so that's how it will stay.'
You then buy a present you feel may please your son,
Seeing it he groans aloud, 'What do you take *me* for Mum?
If I wear that out my friends all will me scorn,
It's ages now dear Mother, since clothes like that were worn.'
Dad needed new socks, you buy pairs in colours bright,
Completely unaware they're meant for cycling folk at night.
He forcefully said, 'E'en in bed, I would not wear those.'
Both family menfolk are putting fingers to their nose.
Sister's getting married wants her niece to be bridesmaid,
Daughter says, 'Not on your life,' and she will not be swayed.
Suddenly Dad comes in and says, 'I am sorry love,
I'll wear socks you bought me, here and out in road.'
Son says, 'I'll wear that gear because it's occurred to me,
I'll be new fashion leader when the blokes that on me see.'
Sister's eyes are shining, happy as all the rest.
Her niece *will* be a bridesmaid now that she has seen her dress.
Then neighbour comes back to say I did that job your way,
It *is* much better method which now I'll use each day.
You've learned to go your own way, it is best after all,
Even if way it first began you really can't recall.

Barbara Goode

The Last Ten Minutes

They'd had their final warning - the 'bomb' was on its way -
There seemed no point in 'doing' - it was the time to pray -
But as they looked around the room -
That might become their living tomb -
They knew that though their time was brief -
It was not the time for tears nor grief -
There were many things that must be said -
To dear ones, who could soon be dead -
Maybe just, 'Thank you for you love' -
Or perhaps, 'I'll see you, up above' -
And all the hate against their foe
Was forgotten now - which seemed to show
That, faced with certain death, men had the will
To really wish for peace - not just to kill.

So, as they waited for their fate,
They realised - though it was too late -
That if ever man was to survive,
All creeds and colours would have to strive
For peace, with just the same intent -
And time, that on the 'bomb' was spent.
But it seemed that every man would have to feel
The touch of death before he'd kneel
To give his all towards the goal of peace -
And only then would wars, forever, cease.

W E & C E Stephenson

IT'S SIMPLY A BRAIN

What is a brain? So hard to understand,
Elegant ladies and gentlemen look so grand,
Music is a draw, a wild terrain on music stand,
Builders they are a puzzle, fearsome band,

Pilot in the air reading dials so bold untold,
Clergy reading sermons to audiences so cold,
Ambulance men on duty, injuries they are sold,
Police's law and order everyone they mould,

Prisoners in jail up and down the land,
People enjoying the seaside walking the strand,
Farmers tending their animals walking their land,
Councillors a funny lot, hard to understand,

Drivers driving lorries all over the land,
Children playing on swings and in the sand,
Sailors sailing the ocean not a merry band,
Soldiers firing guns cannot understand,

People tending animals, selling them for goods in shops,
Chopping down forests making wooden tops,
Laying down pathways seems to go in slots,
Boxers so horrid punch each other till they drop,

Gardeners so busy making pretty things,
Choir boys voices beautiful they sing,
Publicans plying intoxication their thing,
Drugs to the mugs making heads ting,

Factory workers watching machines day and night,
Giving us electric to make the dark light,
Actors at rehearsals not perfect sight,
Vocalist singing scores will they get it right?

The brain is a marvellous thing, versatile, concise,
Writers, poets, can always find something to write.

Derrick Bright

I Was There

The alarm goes off, it's only four
It's dark, it's cold, a chance of snow
Another day six miles to run
Breakfast then off to the gym

Sam is there, he's my trainer
Some exercises then on the weights
Body aches, just one more hour
A quick rub down and then a shower

Weeks and months pass into years
Then the start of all the fears
Didn't do to well last time out
Put it aside, no room for doubt.

A week to go till the next race
It's essential to get a place
Try, try think positive
Nothing else than be first

Ritual each day still the same
In the papers saw my name
I've now become a potential
I've run my first international.

More sweat, more tears, stress and strain
Travelling now by boat and plane
To places of which I'd only dreamt
Now I know what Sam meant.

Eat, sleep and live to train
Improved results will be your gain
Your body must be your temple
Then all else becomes much more simple.

At last my name, amongst the team
I feel better than I've ever been
Win or lose I don't care
I was at the Olympics I was there.

R Middleton

July Landscape In Words

Fields gently falling
Into the valley;
Cottages; farmsteads;
Old grey walls -
Stones piled on stones -
Walling
Pine woods; stately
Fir trees bearing cones.

Ripening corn growing;
Poppies bright red;
Scented wind blowing;
Clouds flying; river flowing,
Pebbles on bed;
A hamlet spread
Over the hillside;
Fresh haystacks in rows;
Cattle in juicy meadows
Satisfied;
Foxgloves in dark woodland;
Ferns; shy rabbits in holes hide -
Just a glimpse of one powder-puff tail
And away he goes
Into the earth to abide.

Mary Richardson

FORGET-ME-NOT

In the stillness of early morn
Where decaying gravestones cast dark shadows
A wild rose prospers
Swaying in compassionate breezes
Listen to the rose leaves murmur
A youthful epilogue.

Only sixteen years of life
Never had a job, there was no work
Just a benefit office, once a week
No money, kicked out of home
For me, a doorway, alley or pavement
An empty belly shrinking
So I begged for money
But more than that
I begged for help
Got a little money, no help
Just blank smiles
Not of understanding
'Next please'

I wasn't a scrounger
Just an outcast, a victim
Raped inside and out
By a civilised society

Old before I grew up
Old in body, mind, and spirit
Then a nothing
A cold body on a cold slab
Waiting to be burned
Then fed to the roses
In the crematorium
So please
When admiring the roses
Spare a thought
For a nobody.

D A Watson

War

Oh! The futility of war.
Fighting and killing
Maimed and broken bodies
Sightless eyes
Grotesque shapes
The smell of death
Sons, husbands and fathers
All gone.
What a waste
Will we ever learn
Or is it too late
Too late to right the wrong
Of wasted human life
Perhaps our children in
Years to come
Will learn from our mistakes
And live in a perfect world
Where everyone is safe

Jean Thorpe

To The Staff Of The RSPCA

I watch this programme every night
And wonder at their awful plight
How could this happen - where's the care
Don't they know God's put them there

Dogs, cats, pigeons, goats and seal
Go to this place for vets to heal
I wish I could adopt them all
Ducks and ponies, horses tall

Their sweetness comes across the space
Loveliness shines in every face
These people dedicate their life
To eradicate the awful strife

Why do people hurt and reject
Should treat our animals with respect
God surely frowns on cruel ways
To mistreat these waifs and strays

Thanks to all the staff who care
To lift these creatures from despair
To make their lives a happy one
To love them all - to give them fun.

Mary Hulme

Roses

We walk in love, unsure
Our path is painfully thorny
Without your love where would we be
Without your strength we'd wither away
Together we stand, divided we fall
Only with God will we stand tall.

Alix Dove (9)

See This Man

See this man I know and love,
He needs motivation, a push and a shove.

See this man with his difficulties,
His innocent mind filled with naivités.

See this man but please don't make fun,
Stop and think, after all,
This man is someone's son.

See this man trying desperately,
To be one of the crowd,
Be just like you and me.

See this man with parents so resilient,
They don't care what others say,
In their eyes their son is brilliant.

See this man he wouldn't hurt a flea
His gentle mind protected, so lovingly.

See this man he needs friends who care,
In the face of adversity he knows they are there.

See this man once known as handicapped,
'Learning difficulties' sounds more humane and
apt.

See this man loved like no other,
That man you see is Malcolm my brother.

Lorraine Hermann

There Is A Little Child

There is a little child
so gentle and so mild,
she waits for me,
to get her tea,
then smiles for all to see.

There is a little child,
sometimes naughty, sometimes wild,
she stares at me,
then stamps on a bee,
then smiles for all to see.

There is a little child,
so innocent and sweet,
crawling at my feet,
she's waiting for a treat,
a sight to behold, a story to be told.

There is a little child,
Heaven knows,
how quickly she grows,
and soon on to school she goes,
a sight to behold, my story now all told.

David Carress

Easter Time

The sadness of Good Friday,
The price that Jesus paid,
Was leading to Easter Day,
When He arose up from the grave.

He rose triumphant on Easter morn
To save us from our sins,
Coming from the churches, happy singing
Of messages and hymns.

Easter - a time for spring-like flowers,
Of lovely golden daffodils.
Sheep with their little lambs on the hills
Are a reminder of the Lamb of God
Who died for us and His powers.

Evelyn M Harding

My Dad

He was a Peter Pan, a child till he died
Children loved him and to them he was an equal
But alas he died after a long dreadful illness
That robbed him of his mind
And no-one recognised the child that was still there
No-one wanted to see him in that state
No-one went to see him in that place
And yet at odd moments lucidity returned
In fleeting words and phrases and then was lost again
Clouded expressionless eyes once more endless repetitive useless
Movements took over once again and father was lost to us
How many deaths do we have to suffer
How many times do we have to grieve
Most people die once, dad died several times in that year
Every time he recovered his memory and lost it
That was to us another death, until finally he really died
Our tears by then were of relief not grief
But we will never forget that terrible year
I sometimes find it hard to remember how he was before
And that hurts even more.

Joan Smith

UNTITLED

My gran laid in her bed,
I walked past to the kitchen,
Water in my eyes they bled,
So poorly she was,
She held on tight,
Everyone but her did fright,
She passed away before our eyes,
There were tears falling
As everyone cries,
There was silence from my mum
For days,
Every wall she looked and gazed,
Not one day passes
Without a thought,
My gran,
Sadness she has brought.

Sonia E J Garforth

FAITH

What is the gift of healing? Is it the gift of love?
Given to someone special and sent from up above?
To those who have the strength of mind the courage and the force
To heal the sick and make their life walk on a different course.
A healing hand can often ease or take away the pain
And give a person hope that life is surely not in vain
I do not know the answer, and I guess I never will
But I know I would be grateful - if I were sick and ill
To know that hands like this are there, my suffering to relieve,
So just what right do I now have to say I don't believe?

L Snow

HAPPY BIRTHDAY OLYMPIC GAMES

War, terrorism, racism, drugs yet the Olympics survive
Testament in itself to man's quest for excellence
The ideals live. For a better world we must all strive
Give everyone a fair go else we cannot know who's best
in the true sense.

Nations here compete in the most important race
To celebrate victory to comfort disappointment,
To make friends learn and understand all members of the human race.
This must be our greatest achievement.

Records are always broken, how far can man go?
Early Olympians could not have dreamed standards of today.
But in getting along with others there is still room to grow,
Hopefully helped along by the physical triumphs on display.

Opening ceremonies grow more wondrous, the right man lit
the centenary flame.
An outstanding athlete of resolute conscience in magnificent physique.
Fought his greatest bout struggling with that shakey frame.
We remember a beautiful smile and not a little cheek.

And now he gives us more, he gives us hope that things have changed
By accepting a gold medal replacing one discarded due to racial
discrimination.
Moronic attitudes have been challenged
And found unacceptable by the community of nations.

We must pay tribute to those who have died at the hand of the coward
And brave spectators who refuse to submit
Lives at risk they march resolutely forward
The games go on the flame stays lit.

Our humdrum lives are enhanced by carnival and spectacle
Founding fathers would be astounded by today's razzmatazz
Long live the most spectacular of spectacles
Long live sport with style and pizzazz.

E McLean

I Would Like To Be

I would like to be a butterfly,
to swoop gracefully on wild flowers,
or flutter by tall buildings
and through open windows
I would settle on a picture frame
to have a little nap.
Then I shall find myself a mate
and in time we shall have some young.
I shall teach them all I know,
to be aware of humans,
who try to capture us in their nets,
or squash us by a newspaper,
powdered and dead.
At night I will fold my wings
and sleep until morning,
how pretty we look
as we awake to start a new day.
The sun creeps out behind snowy white clouds,
while the dew still lays thick on the ground
tells us it's time for breakfast.

M Connolly

Election Time Again

Here they are again,
knocking at my door.
Will you vote for us,
they ask once more.

We can do a lot for you,
they promise at my door.
Will you vote for us,
they ask once more.

You haven't done much yet,
I tell them at my door.
Will you work for us,
we ask once more.

Here we go again,
they're knocking at my door.
Will you go away,
I slam the door.

Anna King

The Race

An expectant hush grips the crowd,
I stand looking round, every nerve tingling,
A voice comes clear, 'Take your marks,'
For what seems like hours,
We wait for the next command,
At last here it comes, 'Get set' and then,
The sound of the starting pistol, echoing in my ears,
The race is on, who will win?
My legs feel like a coiled spring,
Where are the other runners?
Behind me? In front of me?
I see no-one, only a thin white line ahead,
At last the tape is broken,
A roar erupts from the crowd,
But who has won? It's me, it's me,
The strain and anxiety gone,
Now joy and relief, the hours of training,
The hard work and pain, all worthwhile,
As I proudly wear the gold medal.

C Fieldson

What Friendship Means To Me

To me, friendship is forever
Whether you are fat or thin,
Brilliant or stupid
The friendship should always last.

A friend should be someone you can confide in,
And who will be there for you when you need them.

Real friends do not run away when things are rough,
Instead they stick even closer.

All I wanted was a friend,
Instead when things were bad,
They turned away from me,
Leaving me cold and alone
I had so much love to give,
But no-one wanted it.

My love is slowly dying,
My outstretched hands need to be clasped,
Please let me be your friend.

Ms Beckett

Babies

Babies are lovely so full of joy
A beautiful girl or a bouncing boy
Changing feeding by day or by night
The end product is really a sight

Alas they grow up to go it alone
Sometime in the future they each leave home
Sad though it seems a certain light gleams
As they go on their way to follow their dreams
A life of their own that seems to be grand
Miles away in another land

The telephone rings my heart sings
It's bound to bring me joy
With lots of kisses and best wishes
From a beautiful girl or a bouncing boy.

June Christensen

Ode To The Olympic Games

I watched with excitement and baited breath as the
Olympic Games began.
The spectacular opening ceremony the whole stadium rang,
The countries all in their fine regalia and holding the flags so high.
It was so emotional I began to cry,
The swimming and diving were so wonderful but still no sign of gold,
Then Steven Redgrave and Matthew Pinsett, two men so
fearless and bold,
Our first gold medal it was such a joy and with so much pride.
The National Anthem played, the flags flowing in the breeze
side by side,
Then dear old Desmond Lynam said 'Lets go over to the race track'
Now you have Linford Christie and Colin Jackson but there
is only one man, that's Roger Black.
He runs so gracefully and is so fast,
However in his race I closed by eyes and prayed 'Please don't
come last'.
You gained a silver medal and another in the 'four by four',
Mind you in the 'four by one' poor Great Britain dropped the baton
that caused such an uproar
Two weeks and all the events are finished, it all seems so quick
All the long nights watching I began to feel a little sick.
Now to all the people that took part, well done to you all,
And remember there is always Sydney, Australia to look forward to.

L E Schoepp

GOD'S GIFT OF LIFE

To wake up in the morning
thank God I'm still alive
I feel so very lucky
and then 'harder' I do strive

I do my 'prayers and wishes'
and 'know' they all come true
For all the needy people
whose fears are 'never few'

Whatever is their trouble
a fear, or loss of job
I'm someone that they turn to
so let's all join the mob

I get up early in the morning
before my family get out of bed
Pray unto my Master
remember what they said

No matter what they tell me
and no matter just how bad
The Lord in His great mercy
makes bad turn into glad

The 'answer' now is 'simple'
for all you need to do is 'pray'
Yes, the Lord He 'always' listens
be it night or day

So God in all His wisdom
works miracles for sure
So all you do 'is ask Him'
for He will 'know' the cure

Joy Spickermann

WILD FLOWERS

I'll never have all the time I need
To find the flowers that rest,
In varied books, I can't resist
Upon my dusty shelves.
Such miracles of form and grace
The only things that can
Provide us with our staple food
Self-sufficient as they plan.
But every chance I have I go
To search these wild delights
To marvel at their bright display
To admire their persistent growth
On seashore grows the sea kale stout,
Yellow-horned poppies shoot their roots
Deep, deep inside the shingle bank
Under, carpeting sea-pink floor
On shallow pool or acid marsh
Billowing as down, the cotton grass its head
Does shake - a pillow-fight wind-blown.
In limestone pastures, a thistle grows
Carline - when weather's damp they fold their bracts
When dry - open - bees to attract
Wood anemones' petals white
Shyly host in crowds, tall bluebells crown
Their royal heads, in sky-sheeted
Shimmering beam. There won't be time to see
Them all - the millions that all grow
But I will seek and search them there
Until my light goes out.

Joan Richardson

MASSIVE

I'm gonna be massive
I'm gonna be big
I'm doing body-building
and I'm eating like a pig.

I've had lots of protein
I've had lots of meat
and after pumping iron
I get something else to eat.

A mate of mine is massive
he's training like a dog
he eats 12 eggs for breakfast
and spends hours on the bog.

My biceps are enormous
my biceps have a peak
but my legs are really stringy
and look a little weak.

I'm getting really massive
I'm getting really tough
My veins are popping out
but I still ain't bad enough.

Shaun McEwan

NEWBURY

Hot evening - obsolete 'rain', as if told by granny -
Fills with the lunge of hulking youths:
Only they exist for shops' blank reflections.
Others pace warily, guard on defiled pavements
Against ambush, or kiss of bike.

What dog days we've had! How the sweat-soaked collar chafes!
Civility and concentration shrivelled to sharp essentials.
Roll over, grey skies!

A Cohen

The Five Senses

Have you ever wondered
If perhaps a car can think,
Wondering what you're going to do,
Driving it to the brink.

Have you ever wondered
If perhaps a car can feel.
When it gets its offside smashed,
And pain begins to peel.

Have you ever wondered
If perhaps a car can smell,
Humans smoking cigarettes
Within its very bowel.

Have you ever wondered
If a car can see,
Running on to get you home
As smooth as it can be.

Have you ever wondered
If a car can taste,
Well, it can't do everything,
But it can beat you in a race.

Pamela Cooper

TIMEWARP OLYMPIAD

It is 1896, Athens is very still
Here comes the runner
Away over the hill.
His flaming torch is burning
But hush be quiet still.

The pistol gun is firing,
The games have just begun
311 men competing,
Gold medals to be won.

The race is one of courage
The spirit something great
'It's not the winning but
the taking part'
1896 to date.

Athletics, cycling, fencing
Swimming, shooting, wrestling
The noise is very loud
At last the marathon is starting
I cannot hear a sound.
A sea of Olympic runners
Float like a magic cloud
The flame of time is burning,
Spiridon Louis has won
I rub my eyes
The dream is gone
Under the Athens' sun.

M Mullett

LOVERS OF THE WORLD - UNITE

Falling in love, can have a disrupting effect on us humans
Old - lifelong habits, soon begin to alter,
One person only - becomes the focus, of our attention
Whenever - we fall in love, with someone's son - or daughter.

Now - we begin to look at life, through rose-tinted glasses
No more - the harsh reality, of black and white,
No more - that old selfish egotism
No more - that Jack - I'm all right.

Great love stories, have been narrated through the ages
Few more famous - than that of Romeo and Juliet,
Who, it seems - were unfortunate, with their choice of parentage
One - being born a Montague and the other - a Capulet.

Strong family ties, help to keep relatives united
Whether it's Mother and Father love - or a sister - or brother,
Sometimes, a little selfishness tends to cloud the picture
To the detriment of a friend - or would-be lover.

They say - that the course of true love - never runs smooth
But - fortunately, every cloud has a silver lining,
And - if angry words lead to a lover's tiff
The acid test is - how soon will both parties be pining.

So - here is a message, to all those in love
Be proud - your happiness to share,
True love - is like a beautiful orchid
In today's world - it is indeed rare.

Paul Gold

OLYMPICS ON TV

At the moment on TV.
The Olympics are all you see,
They've taken over most of it,
Programmes all had to shift
But for most of us I bet
It's the nearest to sport
We'll ever get.
In our favourite chair
We sit and stare,
Eating and drinking
Maybe a beer or two,
Whatever you fancy, it's up to you.
The winners, the losers
All who take part.
To find fault with any
You haven't the heart,
The trainers, the families
All played a part
Whatever way you look at it
Olympic sport's an art.

Shirley Day

ASIDE WITH GOD

I daily need to set aside
A time alone with God.
A time to read, a time to pray,
And hear just what He has to say.

It takes me time to set aside
My problems and my cares,
So I can come before God's seat,f
Sit quietly at His feet.

My Lord wants me to come aside
And listen to His word,
To meditate on what is written,
And do as I am bidden.

The longer that I come aside,
The closer God will come.
And I'll behold His holiness
And see true righteousness.

Peggy Leach

92240's Story - One Fine Friday

I am a 9F steam engine,
On the *Bluebell Railway.*
Evening Star is one of my kin.
Now one fine Friday
I am by the water tower
Till departure my time I bide:
Third-man puts water in my tender,
A cleaner comes along for a ride.
The driver has gone to get his sandwiches:
So of me the fireman has charge in,
As so in the rules it says,
A senior fireman may within the station margin.
My number is nine double two four zero.
Signalman's given us the lane:
All three in cab, fireman at control,
We cross the points and back onto our train.

Ian, my driver arrives, takes over from Heidi,
She's a woman, as are the other two.
One day she'll be the driver in charge of me.
Maybe I'll have an all female engine crew

Emma Dorothy Shane

My Gifts

I am lucky some tell me
To have so many gifts
Not presents as you may think
Hobbies not just one
I have a stamp collection
Not very big but neatly kept
Postcards old and new I keep
My dolls I love to dress
One Christmas morning when I awoke
I thought of all the people young, old
Who would have one of my dolls
Some would be a fairy on a tree
Some little girls would have one too
Ladies stand them on their dressing table
What a lot of happiness from me

Then comes furniture I love to renovate
Make use of it all over again
My garden I love very much
Slowly it's coming so beautifully
I used to knit but not of late
Then poems I love to write
To a wedding I am going
The bride will read a poem today
One her mum asked me to write
In words her mum was unable to express
So my hobbies I enjoy
Because they too bring happiness
To others when they're feeling low.

Evelyn Farr

Andante

At last! Greet the sun, for the winter was drear.
But the daffodils gleam and springtime is near.
The wind still blows chill yet the heart glows warm
As the burgeoning green works its colourful charm.
The robin is strutting, red waistcoat aglow,
So full of himself as he puts on a show
For his lady love perched on a budding bough.
The voice of a blackbird makes sweetly his vow
O'er the sylvan fields and quiet flowing streams
To keep singing his joy, always filling your dreams.
Sweet harbingers of glories still to be seen,
May we never fail to share in that thrilling paean
Of praise and delight from each living thing . . .
A harmonious prelude to herald the spring.

Evelyn Balmain

The Clubhouse 'Bowls'

The click of woods
            The green of grass
The players, dressed in white.
Down the years, since Plymouth Hoe
it's such a pleasant sight
since Drake first played, the game of bowls
on sward of grassy green.
The comradeship, such clubs can bring
is what it really means.
Cups and such, are nice to win
but really in the end,
it's more that you can enter there
and know you'll find a friend.

Gladys Gayler

EASTER

In Jerusalem crowds gathered for the Passover Feast,
A time to remember Israel's fight for peace.
Jesus rode in under their happy gaze,
The crowd welcomed Him with words of praise,
Spreading palm leaves along His way,
Hoping that He had come to stay.
They followed Him as He cured the blind,
Watched Him healing all the sick He could find,
His words of wisdom they wanted to hear
And He carried on, knowing the end was near.
His enemies too followed, watching and waiting,
Fault would be found, there would be no hesitating.
On entering the Temple Jesus was aghast,
For money changers were cheating those who passed
Through the Temple gates to buy a sacrifice,
Defiling God's House was too high a price,
So in anger the tables were overturned
In the hope that an important lesson be learned.
His enemies now plotted to kill Him,
To betray Jesus, Judas Iscariot was willing,
For thirty pieces of silver his Lord was betrayed
But Judas didn't know the plans that they'd made
And in despair he took his own life,
For he could not live with that sad, dark night.
On the hill of Golgotha Jesus was crucified,
A condemned thief hanging on either side,
He died to show us there is life after death
And asked for our forgiveness with His dying breath.
The true message of Easter is there for all to see:
God's Son gave up His life to save you and me.

Christine Naylor

JESUS CHRIST WAS BORN

Jesus Christ was born, in a stable bare.
The golden star the sign,
the sign that he is here.
And when the shepherds came to pay,
their homage to him that day.
In a manger he lay,
In a manger he lay.

Angels sing his praise, in a rain of light.
Mary holds her child, right up to the sky.
The wise men gave their gifts to him,
the one who will be king.
And reign forever more,
reign forever more.

The spirit of the Lord, is amongst us all.
His voice is calling us, all to his throne.
He came to set his children free,
bore the cross of Calvary.
Almighty powerful Lord,
Almighty powerful Lord.

We are the chosen ones, all over the world.
He is our Christmas gift, for us to be hold.
Salvation is his living aim,
everyone will be the same.
Freedom for everyone,
Freedom for ever more.

Hyacinth Sweeney

Fact And Fiction

To distinguish *fact* from *fiction* is an important teaching task
'Is God a *fact* or *fiction?'* Is something I hardly need to ask,
So many Gods invented by people in the past,
We may be sure the Christian God will not be the last.

The Christian God, invented, PM Thatcher took as *fact,*
And this is why her sacking was a necessary *act.*
But the people left in power in Westminster here today
Are just as *fiction-bound* as she was in her more outspoken way.

If the BBC was *factual* and not *preserving fiction* too,
And not *pretending* to be *Christian, ecumenical* or *Jew,*
They would *reform the whole establishment* to the honest
cosmic creed,
That *people* are the *rulers* and *'God' is dead indeed!*

The whole planet is *'Our Country'*, in this *'post-Christian age',*
This is why a *New World Order* must be *our aim: (agnostically sage)*
We must *teach* new generations the *honest facts of life,*
And *condemn* the *foolish fictions* that around the world are rife.

We must dare to use *democracy* within a global polity,
A Single Global Nation - *United States humanity*
A single global currency, a single phonetic *tongue,*
A single agnostic science faith for *all people old and young.*

That's the way to end all warring and obscene killing acts
Which result from *mis-education* of *fictions* dressed as facts.
We get *'British'* education from the *Cons* as well as *Labs,*
When we need *proper education* instead of *part-world* fibs and fabs.

It is the same in other nations, *internationalism built on lies,*
Where a world of armed nations cause wars before our eyes,
Blame the idolatry of nations which immediately should be,
Deprived of all their foolish symbols of *flags* and *monarchy.*

For *people* are the units in a state that we hold dear,
A *world state* to prevent wars and widespread *human fear,*
Of inter-culture movements which do not know what's *right,*
For *no-one knows* the *cosmic truth* to end our social plight.

Edward Graham MacFarlane

DOES JESUS

Does Jesus walk in meadows
With daisies round His feet
Where buttercups and clover thrive
And springtime lambs now bleat.
And does He watch the rippling stream
In pastures sweet and lush
And see the purple violets peep
Beneath the hawthorn bush.
Does Jesus walk in summertime
And feel the midday sun
And cup His hands to quench His thirst
Where natural springs may run
And will He walk in autumn time
Beneath an orchard fair
To gather apples from the tree
Or seek a ripened pear.
I'm sure He'll walk in wintertime.
Rejoicing in the snow
And feel the flakes caress His brow
Where e'er He chose to go.
For Jesus dwells amongst us still
And knows our seasons well
His presence is forever here
And surely we can tell.

Juliet Eaton

Love Has Not A Barrier

When someone is in love no obstacle can stop him
to go in any direction he wishes to go;
and if anyone will attempt to try they will have a nasty
surprise. The love makes the man feel he is the best.
When you feel the love in your heart then is the time
that you speak. When I had my first love everything
seemed so nice with no cares or problems.
I felt so good and strong, I thought I was the only
happy man on top of the world. But my little
wonderful world did not last for so long. And after
that I had too many ups and downs. But love is
for me always exciting. I would not change love for
any amount of gold in the world. Love makes the world
go round. If there was no love the world will stop and soon
all will be rotten. Love is the most wonderful thing in the summer
and the winter. Love is the fountain of life and we all must try
to drink the water of life. The love and the pain is the game of today.

Antonio Martorelli

The Clouds Cry

The clouds cry whenever it
rains as their tears roll
down windowpanes, but the
clouds' sadness will all disappear
when the sun smiles upon the
clouds and their sadness is no more.

Michael Spittles

HAPPY XMAS - 1990

I've looked and I've looked
But what can I see?
No presents for us under the tree,
No big boxes tied with string,
Nothing to sniff - no diamond ring
No home-made jumper to ram over your head,
Another idea! (Just looked under the bed)

Oh where, oh where can our Xmas prezzies be?

Found 'em.

Both asleep upstairs,
Home-made by you and me.

J Page

THE GYMNAST

The gymnast takes her position.
She cartwheels, triple back flips, she's in the corner.
She dances around the floor.
In her face you see all kinds of emotions.
Concentration, happiness and enjoyment.
She forward flips, does the splits in the air.
She runs and does the finishing tumbles.
It's good, it's excellent.
It scores a 9.875.
The crowd are on their feet.
All except me,
There I sit in amazement in the crowd.

Yvonne Morris (11)

WATER THEMES

Words, words, watery words, washed over pebble dashed beaches,
Until the tide silenced their aching bodies.
And so the dying of Dunkirk lay edified
In a water-filled vacuum - of time immemorial.

These vivid pictures of water washed over
my mind as if to quench my soul.
Like crystal clear droplets that fall so early
In a fine mist cleansing the streets from yesterday's impurities.

Water, just miscellaneous molecules, transient odourless and
yet so pure
Gives life, is life, like the hand that rescues the drowning man
And breathes the purest of perfumes upon the grass.

Can I encapsulate its force in an ecological eclogue
Like a watermill within the stream
Never-ending, turning time, miles into the millennium.

Water, the arbitrator of boundaries, glides and gushes into the sea,
From the river's source or a small rivulet,
Abundant in nature, encompassing an earth with arid deserts.
And yet ambivalent about the route it shall take,
Giving life, taking life, refusing life.

We track it down like hunters shooting wild boar,
But use pipes, valves and reservoirs to store,
To capture a life-giving essence that's essential to all.
We live and we die, and like water we fall.

Christine Flowers

Living In The Nineties

Eastern India, with its teeming millions, must surely be recognised as an amazing phenomenon.

The Samskriti from the seventeenth century states that:
'the forest is the highest form of cultural evolution . . .'
'The forest, in all its diversity, has become the guiding principle of India's civilisation - distinctive in locating its source of regeneration - both material and intellectual - influenced by the diverse processes of the renewal of life from species to species; season to season'.

Likewise, the native American Chief, Seattle, wrote to the American Congress stating:
'the earth does not belong to man, man belongs to the earth. All things are connected like the blood which unites one family. Whatever befalls the earth befalls the sons of the earth. Man did not weave the web of life; he is merely a strand of it. Whatever he does to the web, he does to himself.'

Living in the nineties it is difficult, therefore, to understand
why western countries

'Frankly, my dear, don't give a damn . . .
It's there,
so just enjoy it, man.'

Just *enjoy*, just *live* and *spend* . . .
(Well - doesn't the Bible tell us
'world without end?' . . .)

So live *today; accumulate* . . .
Have it *now* - no time to wait.
Fill trash-cans up to overflowing
Yet - unseeing, and unknowing
Do they know where they are going?

And *they* are the 'educated' ones . . .

Hannah Yates

GRANNY'S BOY

If cheek wi's parcel'ed up for sale
a killing aw' wi'd ma'k nae fail,
ma grandson's got it by the bale
ye'v heard o'w monkeys
he pits the other kids tae' pale,
he's the best for donkeys.

He's only six, but he's got it a'w
he kens the words, and he can ca'w,
his granny's bluff wi' just wa'n bla'w
she's fer' demented
that's why he gi'es her a'w his cheek
tae see her tormented.

His gran she threat'ins him wi' death
she thinks he's got nae auld lip left
then shocks her wi' his very next breath,
wi' aw' toung lashin;
ye wonder how he's lived so long
wi' a'w the bashin'.

She tells him she is in a'w huff
his cheek 'she says' she's had enough,
that's why her voice is harsh an' rough,
but she's only kiddin'.
ther's little or nae response frae him,
the little mid'en.

When he gets in a cheeky mood
an' wants tae wind her up real good,
he'll sta'un an' stick his wee toung oot,
that gets her gau'n
he has a right good laugh at her
she's easy drawn.

But when his gran is going hame
he'll stop his cheeky little game,
an' asks her when she'll come back again
she's first for kissin'
he knows a week's a long long time
for the granny he's missin'.

E S Watson

UPDATE FOR THE ELECTION

If you can trust the Tories when all about you doubt them,
but make allowance for your failing faculties.
If you can force your heart and organs and brain to keep going
though your hospital has been Clarked, Bottomlied and Dorreled.
If you can listen dry-eyed to the community-uncared-for,
those who have lost all and must start again at the beginning.
If you can bear to hear the truth about public services
twisted by smug knaves to make a case for further cuts.
Or talk with the feel-bad poor and not recover some virtue.
Or watch what many risked their lives for destroyed or sold
and ignore the struggle to rebuild despite worn down hopes.
If you can make one heap of all your privatisation winnings
and, not giving any of it away, plead for feel-good tax cuts.
Or walk the streets with waffling, lieaholic ministers
and, tripping over the sleeping rough, not see them.
If, though cringing, you can cheer John Major at Question Time,
or, though terrified, not flinch when Mawhinney tries to smile.
Then yours is the earth and everything in it
(rotting schools; no minimum wage; bloated cats; Tory funds;
sleaze; greed-creed; Scott; poorer poor; prisons boom etc, etc)
and what is more you'll be a true, new, two nation Tory, my boy.

Did someone say 'Nice Mister Major'?

Cecil Bonstein

A Flower

Plucky little flower
growing all alone.
Amidst so much barrenness
What makes you so strong?
'Tis the Father Creator -
who gives me all the strength -
I need. And so I stand and grow -
and grow, for all the world to see.
Perhaps some weary traveller,
passing by, will be cheered on -
life's way.
Upon seeing my glowing face.

N B Mason

Free As A Bird

Gliding through
the open air
sky above
grass below

Ducking and diving smooth as
the ocean,
As white as the snow dashing past me like a flash.

Wings open like loving arms
not a care in the world
Free as a
Bird.

Christina Day

The Awakening

Winter has gone
	and spring has appeared
Let us hope it's a start
	to a prosperous year.

We hope there's no droughts
	nor no flooding of homes
And there is a peaceful solution
	to those wars with their bombs.

We pray that those homeless
	can have their dream house
And that divorces are cut
	between men and their spouse.

We hope that the smokers
	and those drug addicts too
Get rid of their habits
	and start life anew.

Let us create situations
	where there's no further crime
And neighbours work together
	in this moment of time.

Those are some of the symptoms
	that we must discard,
If we are again *great*
	and looked on with regard.

Lachlan Taylor

You Conscientious Worker

You conscientious worker, it's a tall shadow you cast
You are the backbone of the future, like you have been of the past
Eyes wide open, you are on the right course
Beware of those, who will kill a willing horse
You are a gallant soldier, who took charge of his house
You have dressed them in good deeds, both children and spouse
You tend their need, but never their greed
Your offspring have come, from very good seed
Your hands are productive, they are your tools
You walk that line, and never bend those rules
There are no idle hands, to be found in your home
There is not a bad word to be said about yours,
wherever you roam.
You teach them to speak the truth, and never listen to lies
You can walk tall, and can look anybody in the eyes
You are a kid amongst the kids, you have a good time
You nip things in the bud, when they step out of line
You give your love equal, without any shame
If your family bring home strangers, they are treated the same.
Congratulations from the world, and up above
You run your house, on true spiritual love.

Ty Allbright

St Columba Bay

I found a stone upon the shore,
The stone a gift from God.
I roamed hills and dales before,
Ne'er once my foot had trod.

The sounds of waves upon the graves,
Of men who sailed this way.
A number of them were lost,
We bowed our heads to pray.

I have the stone, now in my home,
I found at St Columba Bay.
When in my home alone at night,
I sight the stone and pray.

Christopher R Smith

LET'S CELEBRATE EASTER

Alleluia Easter's here.
Let us all praise God and cheer.
For Jesus you are risen today.
No longer are you hidden away.

After such an unfair trial.
You had to leave us for a while.
Suffered on the cross such pain.
It's hard for us to explain.

Your tortured body on the cross.
Mankind would see the loss,
of such a saviour treated wrong,
and for your presence they would long.

Mary looked at your empty tomb.
Your body was stolen, she did assume.
Joy, oh joy, when to her you spoke.
What deep feelings in her you awoke.

Crucified for our sake.
Oh how much more we did take.
So that our sins may be forgiven.
Your broken body now is risen.

Sue Duckworth

Words

If words could paint a picture
I hope you'll picture mine
I see a field of rich green grass
and many flowers fine.
There's daisies white, and buttercups
give off a golden hue
Purple vetch, poppies red,
and cornflowers of blue
surrounded by a hedge of May.
A blackbird on a bough,
and in the corner of the field I see a
brindle cow.
A footpath leads to distant hills
a cottage stands alone
Sweet-smelling clover by the way
a song thrush to greet me each new day.
If words could paint a picture
a blind man then could see
the beauty of the countryside
that's home, sweet home to me.

Margaret Burnett

Voice

Shout
out
mad crocus
orange-tongued
your six pale violet-veined petals
starring open wide
to clarion the Spring.

Francesca Greene

Black And White Don't Mix, You See

People stop and people stare
Chant hurtful words
They just don't care
We rise above
We keep our heads
We try to conceal
The tears we've shed
Our eyes the same
The same within
The only difference
The colour of our skin
Ignorant of the pain inside
Should we run or should we hide?
It seems that it was meant to be
Black and white don't mix, you see.
One thing we know our love is strong
So how can love like ours be wrong?

Bridget Ward

My Politics

Perhaps I'm too conservative to get involved with debate,
or too liberal with my emotions to configurate,
all the remarkable twists and gaming turns these parties throw,
I could have a major paddy - it's a real labour to know,
which is the best to vote for - it makes no raving loony sense.
Am I too green to decide? Should I just sit up on the fence?
I contemplate and then realise there's no need to be glum,
I could vote for a direct decision - a referendum!

Linda Bagnall

EASTER TIME

What do we mean by Easter
What do we celebrate?
Do we shop and grizzle
How many eggs? Eight.

Chocolate eggs, presents, wine
Everyone here on earth
Going on holiday
Having a good time.

What about the true story?
How Jesus walked on earth
He came to us a tiny babe
Born of a virgin birth.

God sent to us His only Son
To save us from our sins
But how do we repay Him?
We are wicked every one.

Sit back in your armchair.
Say a little prayer.
Thank Our Lord in Heaven
Thank Him for His care.

Read your bible every day
Bend your knee in humble prayer.
Thank Our Lord in Heaven above
He sent us such a lot of love.

Jenny Campling

MOBILE BEAUTY SPOTS

Blunt canyon-wide canons fire a mute salute
Upon the ears of ordinarily runners-from-the truth.
(Evolved with ear-lids) *like*
Our 'I don't want to see,
tell me when it's over' eyelids;
Beknownst not to the flowing molten rock that
sees nor seeks a slave's or sage's path.

The free flowing path of a pure clear stream
Has not a doubt like a lingering dream.
The lava travels no further
than the temperature's vibration *allows,*
And unlike the water
will ne'er look down from the clouds . . .

And glaciers carve paths like streams
but they'll have a *long* wait to
    sprout from fountains . . .
    These glaciers make canyons
    These fountains are the canons
    The eyelids are sand-banks
    The 'ear-lids' are 'What?' 'Who did?'
(Sorry I couldn't have been listening . . .)

Save the streams from freezing.
Save the dreams from retiring.
Save the roots from binding.
Save the banks from sliding,

For none can save the lava from hiding
Lest the retrieving lids seek (dream) guiding.

Lee Martin

Invisible Me

Here I am all alone, but who gives a dam for us
homeless, the infestation living on the roads.
My skin is singed from the cold my body is shocked
with fright, my blanket is the snow, the moon my lamplight.

I once was like you, I too could walk tall, head high in the
sky excepted and respected by all, then suddenly one day the
good life I once had turned upside down left me flat on my back.

You choose not to see me now I'm down on my knees
still you throw me your coins but why won't you see it's
your friendship and help I truly seek.

I remember a time when the world was a sphere of
beautiful colours, people shared with me sincere joy
and laughter, the sounds of nature soothed my inner ear
the softness of the sweet scented breeze stimulated
my zest for life. I wallowed in and out of love and
had friends who truly cared.

Now I don't see or feel these things anymore how can
I see clearly now I'm at death's open door.

Inside I'm still me, I'm still the person I was before
but now that I'm in desperate need who'll help me to
leave the street life this hell that I now call home.

Wendy Forbes

UNTITLED

In front of the gas fire
we become melted cheese
and seep with a stringy waxiness
into the carpet.

The world is woven well
down here and
I can see the telling smear
of the last person you loved.

An insect fights with me
for a crumb, and I consume both
insect and crumb
with my warm width
because I am the blob.

Cigarette ash becomes my eyes and
I'm now going to grow and see
the world down here
for what it is.

The once tacky tendrils
from your blazing orange carpet
are now the twisted pillars
of my fire palace.

The great redwood matchsticks
scorched by the sun
become my giant stilts
and I rise - I rise
to touch the ceiling stars
only to fall like a blob to *earth.*

Martin Nicholson

The Dunblane School Massacre

It came, death's hail, spitting metal, freezing all in its way
their minds still unaware, innocent,
all their attention to gnomes and fairies went;
little did they know, forever young,
age shall never never wilt.

It came, death's hail, spitting metal, freezing all in its way
it all happened in a flash, lightning,
brought all their nightmares to crude awakening;
little did they know, forever young,
age shall never never wilt.

It came, death's hail, spitting metal, freezing all in its way
beware the ides of this century's lust,
for there'll be innocence killed each second passed;
little did they know, forever young,
age shall never never wilt.

It came, death's hail, spitting metal, freezing all in its way
they fell in a swoon, death's gaping mouth,
they shall never know what it was all about;
little did they know forever young,
age shall never never wilt.

It came, death's hail, spitting metal, freezing all in its way
angels were aghast, filled with grief, wrath!
this cruel world spared no-one from shedding blood;
little did they know, forever young,
age shall never never wilt.

It came, death's hail, spitting metal, freezing all in its way
they died for us, we shall always miss,
free to join Rwanda and Bosnia's endless list;
little did they know, forever young,
age shall never never wilt.

Raymond Fenech

THE SCHOOL GOVERNOR

(Dedicated to Marsden CP School, Nelson)

The poor old school governor the person who gives all that time free,
There are about sixteen school governors on a Board,
But only about four or five care and do the work,
The rest just don't care a bit,
It's just a social status symbol to some,
75 percent of LEA governors are a waste or time,
The teacher governors try but fail,
Because of the conflict with staff and others,
The head teacher has a right to be a governor,
The head teacher can't win at all any conflict,
Any complaint the head teacher always takes the fire
It is hard for teachers to keep up with new skills,
When there is no money for training,
No money for children's books some date back to 1960,
In fact schools need more cash,
And over seventeen years of Tories who say they care,
What will the year 2000 bring us,
Will the schools and the NHS go down the drain,
So what's to come, the future looks bleak,
Your school's just fallen into bits,
And when the old school governor looks back,
At the hours of free time he or she has put in,
Will they think it's been a waste of time spent,
After all no-one gives them any thanks,
But a good school governor plods on till when,
He or she becomes old or ill and gives up,
No-one ever says 'Thank you, you cared,'
But you still may have time,
But it's too late for some,
They are now in the grave God bless them,
But at that old governor's rest home,
Just over the hill you still have time to say one 'Thank you.'

Donald Jay

POLITICIANS (GENERAL ELECTION YEAR 1997)

It's that time of year again
When we see the politicians grin
They want your votes
They build your hopes up,
Making promises they won't keep.
They think you have the brain of a sheep.
John Major he knows which side his bread is
buttered on
When was the last time he had to sign on.
Tony Blair he thinks he has the flair
making out he's working class.
He wants to get out and meet
real people on the streets
who have to survive from day to day
on hardly any pay.

Susan Boyle

THE BEAUTY OUTSIDE

The tears dwell upon my eyes
I inhale deeply this vapour outside
Here in the cool early summer breeze
I'm now somehow able to be at ease
To ignore all feelings but those which I have
The want of only nature
But outside this all shows
I shall not want or need to live for
anything else alone
But this beauty outside
That I already own.

Anita Watts

The Village Of Sandhead

When the Lord was busy workin' on our green and pleasant land
And yin nicht, just afore He went tae bed
He was lookin' doon frae Heaven, on a bonnie sandy bay,
And said, 'I think we'll ca' this place Sandhead.

It'll be a peaceful haven, beside the Bay of Luce,
I'll make sure that it's a pleasant place to stay.
I'll make it home for decent folk, the likes of Dr Baird,
And honest workin' men like Jock McCrae.

There'll be Livingstons and Conlays, McCullochs and McLeans
And McKenzies, they can run the village shop,
And in years to come, no doubt, they'll be needin' an hotel,
A pleasant place for travellers to stop.

'We'll call it Tigh-na-mara (the house beside the sea),
Run by a man with charm, wit and fire.
Who better than yon farmer, that farmed at Mulhill,
I think his name was Norman McIntyre'

The Lord, now quite contended wi'the way His plans were going
So cannily He slipped awa tae bed.
But before He slept, He closed His eyes, and said a special prayer
For all the folk that bide within Sandhead.

Harry Monteith

My Love

He was as wonderful as a man could be,
So loving, caring, he worshipped me,
Everything I longed for I found in him,
So tender, warm, a strength from within,
He made me feel wanted, we loved together,
From that day to this, I knew 'twas forever.

Linsay Galloway

News At Ten

News at 10! News at 10!
Is the best news of the day,
When I can put my feet up,
And listen all the way.
Sometimes the news is shocking,
And often very sad,
But then there are items,
Which make you feel so glad.
Next comes the weather forecast,
It is always nice to know,
If it will be windy,
Or rain or hail or snow.
The news readers are very good,
They change now and then,
As do camera-men and others,
Who work for *News at Ten.*

Eugenie Barker

Job Sharing

The market's opened up and now, though unemployment's rife
Britons find themselves under Europe's butcher's knife
Their continental counterparts now taking jobs before
They themselves are even offered foot inside the door
Though politicians still insist on dragging us across
Whilst failing to point out the severity of loss
And mainstream workers struggling send Europe out this call
We haven't enough jobs but come and share them one and all.

Kim Montia

Now Is The Time

Now is the time
Reference the Referendum
Should we? Ought we
To Leave the Common Market?
Do we? Don't we think that
We should make the break?
Everyone must ask themselves
What's best for Britain's sake?
Now is the time to count
The cost of what we've
Gained and what we've lost.
Are we indeed better off
Than we were before?
Someone tell me, tell me do
I'd like to know the score!

S Thompson

Love

Love is a warm glowing feeling.
One is floating on air.
When you are sad and lonely,
Love lifts you out of the depths
of despair.
Love is a bond between lovers.
Promises made above all others,
Only they can share.
Yet, love can grow stale, and boring.
The beauty it once brought disappears.
Then love turns to sorrow and
heartache.
Love brings bitterness,
hate and tears.

Doreen Cox

CLOUDS

The virgin sky glows red with dawn,
Then fades to blue. A day is born.
Bold shafts of sunlight linger where
They warm the earth with tender care,
And water vapour, borne aloft,
Becomes a fragile cloud, and soft
Companions soon form and cast
Precocious shadows when they've passed.

The flimsy clouds go scudding by
Across the lazy summer sky.
They gaily run and fly and dance
And brush each others' sides, perchance
To join together in their flight,
Anticipating coming night
When they, a fluffy blanket throw
Across the sleeping earth below.

As evening falls o'er hill and dale,
To cover all with twilight's veil,
The setting sun, with magic rays,
Illuminates in wondrous ways
The shrouded sky, and in each fold
Plants tiny seeds of burnished gold,
From gold to amber, orange, red,
The pageant passes overhead.

The golden orb at last has set.
A lovely sight to see and yet
Without these streaky clouds of fire,
This splendid scene could not transpire,
And as they wend their skyward way,
Their heaving crests are tinged with grey.
The fire burns low, the embers die,
And darkness now pervades the sky.

Invisibly, the clouds float on,
Their beauty of the day now gone
Alas, and only by the way
They hide the stars do they betray
Their presence in the vault of night,
Till dawn once more, with loving light,
Paints heaven's countenance with care,
And cloudy ribbons in her hair.

Dennis Turner

Blind Love

There's love among the flowers
There's love among the trees
For I know that I can't see them
I can only hear the breeze.

I know that I can touch your face
And feel what you are like
But you can always whisper
And just say goodnight.

Although I'm in the darkness
I can feel my feet on the ground
Just one or two steps forward
Tells me the love I have found.

So please darling just keep touching me
To show that I am here
Then in my darkness
I will show. I will show no fear.

Please tell me all the colours
Of the lovely things
And tell me that you love me
And all that your love brings.

M Stovold

Time Oh Time

Oh time of all things
Of movement
Of patience
Of passing
Oh time of people's lives.
Where we dwell
You are persistent in your
Presence
We can be affected
Like a throw of a dice.
Our mind thoughts are of you
You are man also nature's plan.
Forever moving past forward
We live you to lose you
We are lost
Would not understand.

Victoria Joan Theedam

Nature's Promise

Patterned curtains billow in ever-changing fashion,
As the fresh and gentle wind fans furrowed brow,
And the pure country air, on which there is no ration,
Has caressed our souls from there and then, 'til now.

The mild melodic meadows house many flighted beasts,
Which now hum and buzz, and whine, and keen and drone,
I bask in the sure knowledge that, even at their least,
Each fulfils a worthy purpose of its own.

And when it comes, the rain is not a grievous burden,
But a blesséd boon, sent to ease our sorrow,
A beatific balm, that we may speak no word in
Anger, but trust in promise of tomorrow.

Perry McDaid

MV One

My
life is
like a floppy
disc, I'm a barcode
and I don't exist. Lord
of the ashtray, king of the
roach, I'm tall and thin, beyond
reproach. So hi-tech I'm push button
easy be your role model or a little bit
sleazy. Pseudo saviour, I come in any flavour,
Know all the words to 'Away in a Manger'. I'm witty
and gritty, full of charm, like a nuclear sub that's been
disarmed. I'm stainless and never rust static free and collect
no dust. Pets and kids I just adored, but I can't eat a
whole one . . . raw. I'm the icing on the cake, the
portrait in the Tate, I'm everything you
love to
hate.

Gary Parker

Untitled

The
 Book
  Is
   Open

The
 Page
  Is
   Read

Blow
 Out
  The
   Candle

And
 Go
  To
   Bed.

Philip Allen

News At Ten

New at Ten
The very best
Its presentation fine
The newscasters are on the ball
They sparkle and they shine
And finally - it's over
I'm glad the end is near
It's off to bed I go
A nervous wreck, in fear.

Melvyn Roiter

UNTITLED

Today a whole new way of life, has opened up to me
Exam results are on the 'board' a Staff Nurse I will be
Three years as a student, with lectures by the score
But now all that's behind me, I'll be studying no more
I've been taught to give injections, and administer some pills
I've learned to watch for symptoms, in a wide array of 'ills'.
My main concern is caring, and alleviating pain
To help the doctor put transfusion needles in a vein
Redoing wounds and dressings, straightening up a bed
Dealing with relations, of the patients who are dead
Assisting in the theatres, where instruments are scrubbed
Respecting patients' privacy, who don't want to be disturbed
Keeping charts and case notes, complete and up to date
Making sure that medicines are never given late
The daily round of bed baths, that keep the patients clean
Taking temps and BP's and following a routine
Waiting every morning for our matron to appear
Opening wards for visitors, they bring their loved ones cheer
The list of tasks is endless, but I wouldn't change a thing
The satisfactory feeling of helping people - bring
Immense rewards when on the day, they leave you to go home
Or watch a child get up and walk, for the first time on his own
The pay is poor, the hours are long, I've always got sore feet
But having to do 'paperwork', means I'll get a seat
I don't expect I have a hope, of accumulating wealth
But I have more than those in here, at least I have my health
I've got more responsibilities, I'm now 'second-in-command'
The Sister will be looking, for me at her right hand
To take over when she's on 'days off' or on her holidays
For helping out and taking charge, in lots of different ways
My favourite type of patients are the young and very old
Wee ladies who are kind and wise with stories to be told
Babies are so vulnerable and when they cutely smile
All the hard work disappears and makes my job worthwhile.

Nancy McMillan

UNTITLED

You came into my life
Calmly and placidly
In your undemanding way
Giving of yourself willingly.

You came into my life
Warmly and friendly
Filling my life with meaning
Releasing me from lonely despair.

You came into my life
Smoothly and thoughtfully
Revelling in our closeness
Allowing time to form a love bond.

You came into my life
Completely and entirely
Sharing your precious daughters
Accepting me and my dear daughters.

You came into my life
Tenderly and fondly
Giving me affection and love
Receiving mine willingly and eagerly.

You came into my life
Gently and strongly
Lifting me high in your embrace
Making me content in your presence.

Gill Butt

WHY?

They say there's a reason for
everything in life.
But try to tell that to
a mother and wife.
The happiness she once knew
is gone forever now
How do you explain it
you tell me how.
Resting in some foreign land
For a reason she can't understand
All our dreams are ended
All I have is gone
Why must I be punished
for something I've never done.
Why, you tell me why?

M Thorne

BALLERINA

Your face is always picturesque
Your body held so taut,
The concentration level high
Your mind is clear of thought.
With every step and every sway
You richly glide with grace,
Every move is mutable
As you continue even pace.
Flexibly you adapt so well
A dying swan you can achieve,
You work so hard from start to end
To a polite curtsey as you leave.

Caryne Crane

Peter Our Best Friend

Our mongrel dog Peter was wiry and
Unpredictable right from the start.
He gave so much in time and pleasure
In many ways we were a team, he took part.

Peter aged seven, into every kind of antic
He'd get frantic, be out of the gate.
Motorbikes he liked to chase, or postman
Pat if we clicked the gate too late.

He was black, white and tan, a wild dog
Foot-loose and fancy free
Was humorous, tried his howling act, when
Two girls sang he'd echo as number three.

The one occasion, when stressed by our
Troublesome, but loveable dog
Was a 999 visit by the police shouting,
Torch glaring at a window, in the fog -

Peter kept us on our toes, round the
Garden he would run.
Once he donned glasses, he loved to play
He was therapy, and so much fun.

M Jowsey

Keep A Doctor

A giggle can keep a doctor
Far away from you
And that is how you want it
That is the truth.

A giggle can keep a doctor
Inside his surgery
Only coming out when called
To visit them you and me.

A giggle can keep a doctor
Tied up for a time
But if having fun out of office hours
Whatever is keeping him is fine.

Keith L Powell

New Love

It was the morning after two nights before
I wasn't up with the lark
My head was throbbing, I needed fresh air,
So I went for a walk in the park.
My ears were drawn to jingles playing
And then I heard a tuneful voice
'I'm Ed, the ice-cream salesman
You're really spoilt for choice.
Raisin Rumba, Tropical Tanta,
I can scoop each out with ease
And top them all with sauce and nuts
Or whatever else you please.'
I requested Mauritian Melon Meringue
Covered in long treacle wiggles.
'For you madam, anything. It's coming right up.'
The thought of it gave me the giggles.
Ed stepped out of his van to give me the ice
He reached a magnificent height
His muscles were huge, his smile was so warm,
I believe it was love at first sight.

Sue Jenner

CONCERTO FOR SIREN

From the pavement I hear idling ticking at traffic lights
Then acceleration, gear change pause
Hum and drum of city road concerto.
Soloist enters whirring strident urgency
Rides among them with a surge of revs,
The chunter-along work-a-day vehicles are muted
Hold back respectfully
Their own purposes suspended in rate unity.
He is Apollo on a fiery motorbike
All gladly look to this visible god
White-helmeted and black kitted.
Transcending all - he braves the red
Sweeps into the cross-roads arena
Roars into a magnificent curve
Leans into the turn at speed
The rescuing god daring to balance
On the edge of triumph.
By a modicum of misjudgement
Or a gram of over-confidence
Scales are tipped to gravity -
A crash - percussion - siren ceases.

Lost to view, I picture a mangled mess
Challenge is suddenly thrust at me -
Inescapable beat of a drum
Tortures my conscience,
Should I rush up to him?
What would I do if I did?
Revulsion and duty tug against each other,
He lies sprawled, defeated by himself,
Onlookers are left with stunned emptiness.
A big-hearted lorry driver climbs from his cab
And hurries over. I breathe, relieved.
Miraculously, the patrol man is pulled up
And even wheels his BMW aside,
He confesses the incident on his radio

Stands sheepishly with buckled bike
A show-off schoolboy come a cropper.
Drivers sigh, return to gear
Play their discordant notes again
And disperse in all directions.
He remains dependant, waiting for police help
An unhurt fatality.

Norman Harlington

GROWN ACCUSTOMED (1997)

Currently Prince in England
Future king - privileged road or doomed avenue
My new job, new life
I've already grown accustomed to.

Groomed so, inside and out
My new job - a kingdom - I can face,
More than ready now
My past life I'll have to erase.

'Clocking on' endlessly for
To be a 'bad' king I simply dread
They say don't fret
But *they* don't live inside my head.

It won't be so very strange
Let's face it, it may prove a few more bob
In a way I now
Look forward to my forthcoming new job.

There'll be queries including -
'Which woman by my side' I'm asked - 'Which one?'
Head of kingdom maybe
But still I wonder - has the *heart* gone
(Diana).

Barbara Sherlow

WHY ME?

Why me?
Here I am stuck in bed
with a hot water bottle
clutched to my tummy
and a bottle of painkillers
at arm's length.

Womanhood used to appeal,
when I was an infant
I couldn't wait to be
like my mum.
Now I think how horrendous
it all is. Why me?

It doesn't even stop at teenage years.
The misery will re-invest itself
in older years.
My mother must be on the verge
judging her mood swings.

Why am I irritated
by people who sneer
that pain is natural?
I'll give them pain!

Karolyn Lennon

Shadows Of Solitude

Shadows they show
even in the starving light
of the whitest mid-day sun
They follow me without respect
constant companions
They just stick to my heels
and phantom my steps
Outlining and feeling
their concrete way
as I amble aimlessly
Ghostly they trace
where I am heading
knowing my direction
before I
Anticipating each
printed footfall
with a toe-hold on my advance
Tracking my future - making full -
Circling like buzzards
through the progressing day
I am the dial and my shadow
the hours and the days
just sweeping away
And when I finally lay down
and no more shadow is cast
The moon will shine a path
of solitude and loneliness
but with a beauty
which eases all pain.

Jack Insch

THE ROAD HOME

A horrified look appeared on my teacher's face
when she heard me say 'It's a poem about cocaine.'
It was as if she thought I had been doing a vanishing act
with lines of Bolivian marching powder on the table.

I felt like saying the table was the wrong colour, but I
didn't think that she would have found it very funny.

The smoke-filled air round the big white building near the
games-field filled my lungs like a poisonous gas rising
from the explosion of a chemical plant. I felt sick as
the smoke from their half-burnt cigarettes filled
the air around me. The clear air ahead of me becomes
a great relief as I have passed the smoke that surrounds them.

Teenagers with a death wish. A large green area surrounds me
as I turn the corner but I am soon to be surrounded by buildings
housing ignorance.

Mark Bateson

THE COUNTRY AIR

The lovely flowers and beautiful trees
Sway like a whisper in the breeze
The sweet scented lilacs blossoming out
The hums of the bees, the splash of the trout
The trickling waters that flow on their way
The smell of the grass, the wind and the hay
The taunting aroma that gathers around
From the birds in the trees to ants on the ground
These pleasures submitted to our request
And hope we will follow to do our best
To enjoy all things that we have day to day
And happily merrily go on our way.

Taryna Bradford

The Whole Thing

The variance of nature,
bright colours and even slime.
The glorious hue of the parrot,
The slug on its slippery climb.

The highest mountains.
The lowest vale.
The feather and skin.
The hair and nail.

Something dead,
but continually growing.
Something static.
Something flowing.

Something that talks.
Something that whistles.
Things that flower.
Weeds and thistles.

The snake and fish.
The elephant and whale.
The largest to the smallest.
The worm, ant, and snail.

Dog and cat, mouse and rat.
The goldfish in its bowl.
You and me, the sky and sea.
Nature contains the whole.

Ted Harrison

I Do Despair

Your light pouring into me,
Filtered through stained glass
And dispersing some shadows,
Is what has moved me most.

Your colouring liquid
And penetrating pigment
Has mixed with my own
To create a new transparency.

It has helped me to see
Differently and to pass
Through the darkness that knows
Your all-too-familiar ghost.

All that I previously hid
Is now revealed in a new firmament
In which emotions have grown
With a mental and moral urgency.

I have felt our flickering souls touch
Like a butterfly's wing stroking the air.

I love you so much
That I do despair.

Bob Crew

Dad

One day my hand got too big to be comfortably lost in yours
and I found that I could cross the road on my own anyway,
so it didn't matter.
Your hand was callused and too rough to feel properly
but you wore the roughness like a badge or tribe or identity.
A member of the lost tribe of the north.

Then my hand got even bigger,
too big even for the factories and workshops
and the drizzle that hung in the street-light and gritstone gardens.
I became known as 'Lad who went to college'.
And you changed into 'Sick, terribly sick',
and eventually 'Gone'.

I'm still trying to pinpoint who I became at the end of the day,
it's hard to be sure when there's no-one to compare with.

Colin Duffield

A Day In March

Families with pushchairs on neighbourhood strolls
With little girls skipping ahead as they go.
Ladies in gardens sweeping the drive
While men with machinery service each part.
A sports-car drives past with top folded down
Stereo playing some unidentified sound.
Bicycle children make rules for their play
To escape a monster just beamed here from space.
Cars being cleaned and hedges pruned
While birds in the tree-tops sing joyful tunes.
Then the sight of a butterfly flitting its wings . . .
Confirmed by Mother Nature 'tis the first day of spring!

Brian Couzins

THE BLESSING

By osmosis the blind man reads the day
Tasting colours in the wind and air
Hearing whispered secrets in winding mist
The permeating light and peace absorbs
Bestowed by morning's gentlest gift of warmth

Blessed angled contour, limber limb uplift
The flesh alert to lightest shift and list
Within a limpid soul that lives in trust
Response and correspond, man to dust
Expanding joy, give thanks, unite
In kirlian incandescent light

The mood, meaning, hue and scent of day
Arrayed and ranged in riot, a syrinx play
Excite delight and fill, a rising ancient instinct thrill
Primordial reflex start
A keen, sharp, phlemen art
As honed as any predatory skill

No pity here to poison gifted heart
With sightless words that prove dull counterpart
For one that ventures, welcome, wooded paths
The deepest recess, forest chamber
Secret, pulsing, hallowed hearth.

Janina Mszanska

Country Matters

You won't find me where the scenery
Is half hidden by the greenery,
Walking down a leafy lane
Only to walk back again.
Joining others on a hike,
Pushing pedals on a bike,
Trying to make the wheels go round
Merely to observe the ground
Covered with a lot of weeds,
Shaking all their little seeds
Blown like an army of marauders
All over my herbaceous borders.
When it rains there's no shop door
For shelter. There should be a law
Against it raining out of town
When absolutely hissing down,
And one to stop the cows from mooing,
And stop whatever they are doing,
There in the fields for all to see.
It's such a frightful liberty.
Spring is only good for cleaning,
Summer only brings the flies.
The flower that makes it without wilting,
Autumn makes damned sure it dies.
Winter brings the Christmas snow
And frost that people pray for.
It turns to ice, and falling down
Is all that it's okay for.
Nature is unnatural, I've little doubt of that.
If you can find a better place than home,
I'll eat my hat.

Cy Smith

Centring The Universe

In a traffic-circled square,
beneath Nelson's battle-blinded eye,
canopied by a kingfisher sky
we confess desires and find they marry.
Human-hungry pigeons peck our toes
eager for the crumbs of our benefice.
Voices, foreign and harsh, spin webs of sound
but we, honey-throated and hushed,
speak only the language of love.
The air, exhaust-laden and tired,
slinks into our lungs and emerges
refreshed,
cleansed by our happiness.
The September sun blazes,
bold, bounteous and brash,
reflecting the fire of our passion.
Fountains sparkle and surge
aping our exuberance.
Echoing the lions' pride
we know the world spins at our behest.

Beneath the surrendered eye
of the conquering hero
we surrender I
and become inviolate.

Susan Fincham

Death

The loss of a loved one, oh so dear
Has brought us pain in this sad year.
But we know You are working out Your plan,
When we put our lives within Your hand.

Lord, only You know the pain and fear
Of losing a loved one so dear.
Only You know how we feel
When our hearts within us peel.

It's hard to think that those you love
Should suddenly depart,
And leave you wondering why
They left us all with such a start.

Only You, O Lord can know
The reason for and why,
These loved ones should be called
Home to You . . . to die.

But only for a moment,
Then with You they reign again.
And with You there in Heaven,
They know no hurt or pain.

Please keep us ever close to You -
In all we say and all we do.
And teach us through Your word each day
Just how we ought to live and pray.

Christine Surgenor

A Sad State

Politicians are people who rave and shout,
Now we are in, try getting us out.
You tried the others, they were no good,
As thick as two planks, or pieces of wood.

Just look what you have since we've been around,
A National Health system run into the ground.
Then there's the pits, we are closing them down
Shutting our eyes to the miners who walk around the town.

The schools and the colleges, new tests they will get,
It turned out to be the biggest bodge-up yet.
To solve this problem they worked all night,
Then decided all children must first learn to read and write.

Your fuel bills will be cheaper we made sure of that,
You cannot afford it when we add on the VAT.
Just put on your coat, pull your collar up higher,
While I put another log on my fire.

The trains and the buses, they never pay,
Never mind, we will soon be able to give them away.
All the main services went like a bomb,
We even gave them money to help them along.

The unemployed, sick and old,
Are where we want them out in the cold.
Your money we've spent, we have not a clue,
Good luck to us and bad luck to you.

So remember when you go out and vote,
Be it for a young man or a silly old goat,
Everything will remain the same,
All you have done is change the name.

The safest bet, if you want to win,
Is pick your candidate out with a pin.

B A Plumb

Save Us From Political Rhubarb

Surely those in Parliament should set a good example,
but what they keep on dishing out, is not what we should sample.
On telly and on radio, they can be seen and heard,
calling Rhubarb, Rhubarb, it seems their favourite word.

They call Rhubarb, Rhubarb, Rhubarb, ain't they got no manners?
They get a fair bob for the job, though some ain't worth old tanners.
Instead of finding jobs of work for all the poor have-nots,
they're there with enough Rhubarb, to give us all the trots.

Some in The House of Commons, are a right common lot,
they keep on Rhubarb, Rhubarb, and give it all they've got.
Now sensible debating, is nothing but a sham,
with all that Rhubarb, Rhubarb, they just get in a jam.

Even the so-called upper crust can not leave Rhubarb out,
it's plumfully pervasive, in whisper and in shout.
Whatever their persuasion, they'll Rhubarb as they dream,
they should get covered in compost, with custard, or with cream.

Rhubarb relieves the tension, and stops them getting bored,
they think a well-placed Rhubarb, has more points than the sword.
They can't touch them for Rhubarb in parliamentary frolics,
that's why they all shout Rhubarb, when what they mean is 'different'

Now they televise them, and transmit them to our homes,
surely they are as welcome as headless garden gnomes,
but if it stops their Rhubarb, that would be just the ticket,
when Rhubarbs plea, please vote for me! Let's tell them where
to stick it.

John Manning

Don't Tread On Me

I'm a scorpion
Don't tread on me
You might feel safe
But just wait and see!

I'll give you passion
Affection and love
Don't take advantage
And I won't get fed up.

If you think that you've got me
Locked up in a cage
Watch out for the sting
Of a scorpion's rage.

I'll sit patiently
To see what arises
But if you tread on me
You'll get some surprises.

Not many people
Get the sting of my tail
It's sowed for the ones
That miserably fail.

Martine Flack

The Secret Vote

On polling day a fine blue car
Purred gently in the street,
Come to collect my granny
And save her weary feet.

Her neighbours, nosy, later
Said 'We saw that posh new car!
Who was that who was in it?
Where did you go? How far?'

And still they kept on saying
'Come on, Lil, what's the story?
How come you got a car like that?
You've *never* turned a Tory!'

Lil said: 'Some kind folk offered me
A lift. I should not gloat.
But I knew they'd be too polite
To ask me how I'd vote!'

Penelope Alexander

Gambling Man

I strolled past the bookies, one fine day,
hadn't in years, walked that way,
turned my head, recognised a face,
he looked tired, drunk, a disgrace,

So I called his name, we sat,
talked, shared some cheap wine,
he told me his story, one of love,
an old chair, TV, bottle of beer,

He had a small business, selling cars,
beautiful wife, a child, nice life,
he sold a car, it killed three people,
soon after, he took the bottle,

I asked, if he knew the brakes were faulty
his reply, was yes, I asked why,
took a chance, the odds were even,
I can't help it,

I'm a gambling man

David G Teakel

Hearsay And Hate

He came here in old age perhaps rather late
And found his name smeared by the jackals of hate
Who spread their hearsay
While telling the old
Don't speak to him
Just do as you're told.

I've heard he is evil
It must be true
And I don't want to see him
Ever near you.

But the spiteful tongues have had their day
Although it never really goes away

Because the name of the game is hate.

D S Hussey

Love

To know is to want
To want is to love.
To the infinite infinity to love.
As the tearing motion of a crashing wave
Crush me in the depth of your desire,
Pull me to the whirlpool of the deeps
Tangled with swaying weed
Slimy and wet as my femininity
Strong is the underflow of my love
As the currents of the cruel sea
Violent in the ultimate strength
of a terrible stillness
My heart beats as continuous as
the movements of the ocean.

Heather Tweedie

NATURE'S FLAG OF WARNING

The topaz gleams
Between parallel jet.
Ruler-straight lines
Of startling colour show
Nature's flag of warning.

Mother Nature's best display
Of colour-coded clothing.
Dangerously handsome,
And with impeccable style,
He goes about his business.

Muttering under his breath
In monosyllabic tones,
He expresses irritation.
Which turns to frenzied anger
When a target blocks his path.

In pristine uniform,
And with intimidating words,
He confronts the enemy.
Glaring with menace;
His weapon well concealed.

He avoids with artful agility
Opponents' defensive blows.
Weapon penetrates victim.
Haughty and arrogant with triumph
The wasp glides away.

Peta C C Vale

What Love Has Made

Where the world revolves around you
I see alone where I have fallen
Where the sea claws at the sands
Falling inside of me in our time spent
Our hands a knot of thick rope found
And what it meant, aside of sound
Hushes of the surf that disappears
On horizons never near to me
Held so dear to me, so dear to thee

Where the world stops here around you
Rope we find and hope to cling to
Unravelled in our desperate hands, once caressed
Smooth golden sands, clawed and scratched
What neither shall keep, but give away our love complete
And find us here always looking for each other
When we are not alone looking for ourselves.

Malcolm Andre Penny

Awakening

My mind awakened to the call of the blackbird,
His voice so shrill, so long not heard.
The long winter days and nights so cold,
Had passed as spring announced itself too bold.

Away in the distance the cuckoo chants,
Which starts in the spring, to us it grants,
The regenerative time that nature unfurls,
And animals' hibernation will slowly uncurl.

A bird that has been with us all winter long,
Is the robin so cheerily always on song.
Will stay about while we turn the soil,
Watching the worm from nature's toil.

As the earth revolves and the mornings get lighter,
The world in its glory lifts its head and looks brighter.
The leaves on the trees and the bulbs in the ground,
Peep out as if to say, look about, God's wonder is all around.

Valerie Marshall

Spring Is A Joyful Caper

Birds come with the light
Of a new day begun
Radiant rascal
The sun
Ball-bright
Crashing through window
To land in my room
With fiery fingers
Bids cherry trees bloom
Later much later
The counterpart moon
Hangs high
Pale-ivory globe
Rides out the sky
Shakes free of cloud wisp
Veiled lace
On her face.

Jean Holt

THOUGHTFUL KATE

Please do not think that all;
who do not marry,
Are unable to find a Tom,
A Dick, or Harry.
Nor is it ambition,
Or a parent's cry for help,
Or giving preferential treatment,
to a family member over self.
Nor prudery either, that builds
resistance to the twinning state,
It is the lack of Bull-dog breed,
deterring thoughtful Kate.

With fear and avarice now,
our humble lives are sated,
Sadly our homes must now
be locked, and barred and gated.
Men who we elect to guide us on our way,
Do blather on endlessly and,
unfortunately have feet of clay.
Unable to give up privileged living,
and return to basics.
God's commandments show the way,
no finer set of ethics.
Jesus fed five thousand with
two loaves, and five fishes,
Pie in the sky is offered today,
but not in dishes.
We rage and complain,
someone must take the blame,
But the smoke goes up the chimney,
Just the same . . .

Margaret Bailey

HOPE

Dawn follows the darkness of night
in the morning there is light
As the sun sets the moon rises
these are not all surprises

Easter is not just hot cross bun
and everything that is fun
It is not all coloured eggs
and chocolate eggs

Easter is our reminder
that our sadness we can put asunder
The sadness of Good Friday
forgotten on Easter Sunday

The beginning of a new hope and glory
as told in the Bible story
For each and every death
there is always a new birth

As we bury our dead
think of it as putting them to bed
on their way to Heaven to meet Our Lord
they will be happy there with God

Our time here on earth may be out
In Heaven by God Our Lord we will be met
A new life out there awaits us
And Our Lord will always abide with us

Easter brings us hope and happiness
to retrieve us from our sadness
Christ's rising is our celebration
for believers to sing in jubilation.

Albert Moses

WILLIAM, HURT

I walk by the kissy tree
Here like an accident
Where I don't belong
This was the place where we said hello
Where I had come to write
To have thoughts tumble out of my head
Onto the page
Disjointed and unconnected
Merging into a rage
If truth dictates a romantic soul
I thought myself
The least romantic soul on earth
For I had lied to ensnare a heart
She had discovered this
Said we had to part
So I came here
To console myself with words
Then I saw you
Simple and elegant
And exciting and delicate
Let me love you
Let me care for you
You and only you
I saw you and I wished
You seemed alone as me
So I went to speak to you
We engaged in company
Linked our arms
An affinity in infinity
And we loved
Though it was many years ago
Our time was brief
How could we know
How weak your body was
How fragile you were
How little time we had to love

Sally was her name
She captured my heart
Her natural beauty
The perfect compliment to the park
All these thoughts
Come up in a second
As I watched the women come and go
And I remembered what I had buried
Laid to rest with you
I thought in time I could visit this place
But without you
I just don't belong
By the kissy tree.

Lee Ryder

DAUGHTER'S LOVE

Some months have gone by since my mother passed by.
When I'm asleep she is there.
When I'm sad she is there.
We talk not mumble.
We laugh not cry.
I've pushed her around in her wheelchair.
Oh how I struggled with my stick.
Some days she was happy, some days sad.
When I was a little girl she tied my shoe.
She parted my hair, she bought my dolls to put in my pram.
She helped me to dress and say my prayers.
I loved her, I kissed her, the smiles I'll cherish.
Her ring on my finger gives me peace and pleasure.
Dad gave it to her on her wedding day.
A pride in Heaven she will stay.

Jean Rickwood

SPRING IS . . .

Winter has almost gone
 A new spring has sprung,
Our feathered friends are daily visiting,
 The glorious colour of our flowers
Hedgerows too are beginning to awake
 The rich yellow of the daffodils the snowdrops so serene
A little cluster of primroses peeping as to say
 Spring is truly on the way.
Let's not think of the dark dull days
 Just keep on looking for each delightful bud to appear
And say this is a violet to enjoy today.
 What next tomorrow, we shall see
The hedgerow has so much beauty for all of us to see
 The baby lambs are so much fun
Do stop a while and watch mother and child
 Each sharing such love and gentle caring.

Norma Pusey

NO TITLE, NO LIFE

To lay in a doorway
To not have an address
What has my life become
 except a bloody mess

The Social will not house me
I cannot find a job
The looks I get from passers-by
They think that I'm a yob.

No money, no life, no self-respect
When will all this lot end?
To live each day from begging
From strangers I depend.

The dreams I had when I was young
The streets made them disappear
To think about my future
I can't I'm filled with fear.

Lesley Jane Gammon

Mum

I'm always here for you if you need me,
to cuddle your pain away.
I promise never to leave you.
They say out of sight out of mind,
but they've got it all wrong.

I may not be mature enough to understand
the full responsibility of being an adult,
but mum I'm still a teenager.

You don't need all the grief and pain,
I'm sorry I started it all again,
I hope you can forgive me.
I've paid for my mistakes,
and believe me I have learnt from them,
I love you and although you think
I'm not old enough to understand,
I'm old enough to know how important you are,
I hope I grow up like you.
My mum.

Bonnita Goulden

FARMYARD BLUES

One night I had this mixed-up dream
That all animals I had seen
They got their lives in a muddle
So strange, so weird, oh fuddle duddle.

The cow she sounded like a sheep
Wandered off, to find little Bo-Peep
My old cat barked, my dog he neighed
What a strange way for them to behave.

It's funny now that I think of it
A mouse burrowing a hole almost like a rabbit
With wriggling ears both look the same
The miracle of dream that's who's to blame.

It was so much fun when this dream begun
To watch the hens jump over the sun
It should be the cow jump over the moon
And pigs were flying all around the room.

A fish who climbed to the top of a tree
Then buzzing around just like a bumble bee
The big white swan, and a little grey duck
Were sound asleep in a rabbit hutch.

The midnight owl was swimming in the water
Far away on a hill top I saw an otter
This magical dream had come alive
Old crow was sitting inside the beehive.

The snow was falling it was winter time
From beyond the clouds the sun would shine
I looked out of the window and I saw a goat
Sailing down the river on a motor boat.

Hedgehogs having fun in the old pigsty
A dream's only a dream as time goes by
Horse was in the stable singing a 'la-la bye'
All the beautiful colours of a butterfly.

When at last I eventually awoke
I thought a frog was stuck in my throat
I sat for a while feeling so blue
This lovely dream if it could only be true.

The trees talked and squirrels squawked
In this dream of *only make-believe*
As lambs bathed silently in the garden pool
I'd better get ready, it's time for school.

Graham Macnab

THE FLOWERS THAT BLOOM

O Lord I love the flowers and the brightness they show
As I look at them standing all there in a row
They shine and do tell us of the love that you give
You give us in plenty
So that we might live -
Live in your love and worship you O Lord
Thank you O Saviour for being our Lord
Flowers that bloom do tell us each day
Of your love that blossoms in our hearts day by day
Day by day and hour by hour
You send us your love in each flower
With heartfelt thanks we cherish that love . . . we receive
And we say . . . to you - O Saviour
Our hearts do believe . . .
Our hearts do believe . . .
As the flowers that bloom in Heaven.
We do believe
Amen.

Val Backs

KENSAL GREEN CEMETERY

One Christmas Eve I ventured forth from Grays Bookbinders,
Intent on fulfilling only my deliveries
And going back to hearth and home.
But I drove to a place I had not been,
The cemetery that lies at Kensal Green.

What gates! What Gothic splendour!
Winter's presence closed me in just like a fog I could not dodge
As I took that leather-bound register into the keeper's lodge.
I looked around gazing at a world so different from mine,
A place where winter's presence helped freeze the march of time.
I could have been a frock-coated gentleman
As I surveyed a view fully Dickensian.

It seemed fitting I should be delivering for Headley Molinyeux,
A name Dickens himself might have used, reminiscent of
a character or two;

Like that poor demented Bradley Headstone
Or Lizzie Hexam's love for Eugene Wrayburn
Or Pip crouched in terror by his mother's grave
Unaware of great expectation?

I left this other world not knowing I would pen this page,
Aware I had stepped back in time to feel a bygone age.

Jack Flowers

THE NIGHT SKY

The night sky,
stretched out before me, like a blanket of blue,
whilst stars scattered, look like tiny pearls.
I take a deep breath, the air fresh, clean,
my lungs seem, as to sigh,
for this gift of nature, that man, so often pollutes.

The temperature cool, giving the air a slight crispness.
I can see my own breath.

Sitting for hours, I watch the coming of dawn,
and hear the first notes of birds' song,
and the first dew to form on young, innocent leaves.

The fragrant flowers, give off their early morning scent,
as their bright petals open up to the morn,
as like a virgin, glowing in the first taste of true love.

Oh, what wonders these are, that nature gives us,
without doubt it is a glorious world.

Raymond Mandeville

HAPPY NEW YEAR

Christmas comes and goes
Oh, how cold our toes!
New Year is waited for
In anticipation
We put our trust in God
Who always 'gives the nod'.
At something good.

Jean H Davy

To You - My Secret Fantasy

My fantasy, who are you?

Although I know your face,
And I recognise your name,
I've never even met you,
You've set my heart aflame.

Maybe because I can't,
It makes me want to touch you,
And feel you in my arms.
Or just because I shouldn't,
Even see your charm.
The beauty in your eyes,
And a smile so strong, yet with a tenderness,
That remains in my heart,
And always in my mind.

Everything I feel for you,
Is what I'm told is wrong,
It goes against the rules,
But maybe that is half the reason,
I feel the way I do.

But if I ever met you,
would I still feel the same?
Or is this just a fantasy,
that's best left in my head?

Claire Marie O'Connor

WASTE

On street corners they stand
Lamp-posts prop up,
Merry little bands
Canned fizzy drink sip
School dull?
Why go
Joy riding a pull.
Panda car in tow
From supermarket nick
Brick walls, graffiti spray
Authority lick
Parents to neighbours exploit relay:
Regardless of health
Syringe, reefer, pill
Used in stealth:
Quick theft, confound the 'Bill'
Aged molest
Declining years haunted
With interior unrest
Culprits o'er fence vaulted,
Neither sense nor reason
Behind brutal acts,
In and out of season
When all must exercise tact!
Police caution, pop in cell
Familiar as home
As all can tell,
From miscreants' tone,
Time, so precious a gift
Improperly used, abused, a waste.

Nora M Davidson

Shopping Centre

Shopping women have more than their share of
ordinary faces
and splendid legs.

They have more than they deserve of
ordinary husbands; though mostly
they don't seem to have husbands
                    but walk in pairs
bird-ankled and rapier-heeled
an inch or so above the street.

Their outfits, on the whole
tailored, casual, tasteful, elegant
suit any one of the others passing
better than them.

          As though they knew
they had made the last choice wrongly
and would choose wrong again, their quick step
carries them to the next boutique
discreetly decked with fashions and mute appeal
and raging indecision.

Roland Portchmouth

My Mum

My Mum looks like my brother.
My Mum smells of perfume.
My Mum feels like a lamb.
My Mum sounds like tins
                crashing down.

I love my Mum.

          Love from Jake

Jake Gordon (7)

EASTER EXUBERANCE

What is of importance at Easter time?
Rolling boiled eggs down a steep incline.
Shells brightly painted, to represent a clown's face.
Happy is Larry, if he wins the race.

Relaxing pleasure breaks at this holiday season,
Occupies the mind with exciting reasons,
To frolic on the beach, paddle in the sea.
Flying a kit, or exploring a festooned quay.

Munching Easter eggs, oozing with cream.
Tentatively, holding baby chicks, entranced by their appeal.
Ripping open an envelope with excited haste
Revealing an Easter card, denoting God's grace.

As we savour these seasonal, delicious sweets,
And enjoy these activities, occupational feats.
We are reminded of a historical important event.
When Christ rose victorious from the tomb, over death.

We celebrate His resurrection, on Easter Day.
Christians have personal experience, so they know He's the Way.
His truth is relevant, from birth through to death.
We will live forever with Jesus, when we leave this earth.

Live a 'new life' in Jesus, each moment, each day.
He's our glorious hope, amidst affray.
Christ has ascended, and He bids us come
To join His redeemed, around God's throne.

Meanwhile, we're commanded to speak His truth.
Witnessing for Christ as true followers should.
His indwelling power, transforming our demeanour
Vigilant for Christ, like a effulgent flower.

Easter is special with God's message of love.
Reaffirming His care, towards inhabitants on earth.

I Rosie

CONSCIENCE MONEY

Raindrops falling through the darkness
Empty faces in a crowd
Lonely people in desperation
Angry voices shouting loud

Crying babies, hungry children
Screaming out for scraps to eat
Frightened bodies wanting freedom
Broken shoes upon their feet

Starving, lying in the gutter
Forgotten lives we pass them by
Do we care enough about them
Or do we speak another lie

Drop some coins in the collection
To keep our consciences at bay
In our lives of joy and plenty
As we smile through another day.

Talking of the sad and lonely
But hoping they won't pass us by
Leaving us to view at distance
Because it makes us want to cry

Afraid that this might one day be us
Begging for our daily bread
Needing someone else to feed us
No comfy place to lay our head.

Elizabeth Hobson

Living Too Long For The Economy

I grew old
In the Tory kingdom
And never thought to see
A life that slowly offered
Lean purse and fat anxiety
For politicians have a game
To lie the truth they play
Their bets are hedged
It matters not if there be disarray
Expect from me for living
No payment of a fee
My birth date 1920
Is long past history
Life flows along
In turn will you
For living pay a fee
Or sing a different song?

Jean Holt

A Valentine Frae Yin OAP To Anither

'Ma mooth is like a rosebud,
bereft o' flashin' fangs.
Ma bum hae drapped a wee bit,
an shoogles where it hangs.
Ma boobs resemble coo pats
That skitter'd on the gress.
Ma legs they are gie shoogly
as they dangilt 'neath ma dress.
But a hope ye overlook this
When ye gaze intae ma een
An see reflected luv there
Fur you ma *Valenteen!*

Maggy McGhie

One Man's Naval Experience

I joined the Royal Navy for a briny life at sea.
I didn't think of anything 'cept a matelot I would be.
I'd pull the ropes. I'd pull the girls.
I'd visit foreign climes.
That salt sea air would give me curls;
I saw nought but happy times.

Reality soon would rear its ugly head,
Attacking all on which my dreams had fed.
No ship for me: but barrack square
Confronted me at first.
A brutal gun'ry PO stood there
And my every step he cursed

'Left, right, left, right; right wheel!'
Was all he seemed to shout;
And, when I'd mastered that, he made me turn about.
When I changed my step into a camel's march,
He cast doubt on my parents' bond,
He was hardly the kindly patriarch
Of whom I might grow fond.

Eventually they gave me a ship,
The staid old KGV,
Whose only trusted sailing trip
Was to some seaside dive.
We showed the flag in old Torquay,
Along the south-west coast,
And let the trippers come on free
So they could forever boast
They'd been on board an HM ship that had sailed the briny sea.

A gunnery course I was offered
After a few years at sea:
But a glance at all the options showed
Nought to int'rest me.
Till a notice I espied, down in the mid-ship flat:
'Be a naval airman' - I thought I'd like a taste of that.

So, to naval air recruitment, I soon was on my way -
To a barracks down in Gosport I arrived that fatal day.
We seemed to do the same old drill with rifle, boot and gaiter,
Which only fed my tendency to be a PO later.
Instead of aircraft carriers, across the field we'd trek -
To practise hook-releasing on the concrete dummy deck.

When, finally, we went to sea
On board a carrier vast,
Another curse confronted me
In this role I'd been cast.
Beneath the decks, our living space
Left much to be desired,
There could not be so poor a place
To return to wet and tired.
At night we slung our hammocks high,
Hemmed in all the while,
With bods enough to make you cry -
I scarce could raise a smile.

From then on, till my blest release,
My naval shocks would never cease.
I found I could neither bend nor hitch,
My inadequacies had reached a pitch
Where chief and bosun saw me as
A sailor who would never pass
To PO's rank, or even lower.
(I was, also, a lousy rower.)

When, finally, I had earned my Burton suit,
In which, Ma said I looked 'quite cute',
I realised what must be - must be:
A sailor's life was not for me.
I decided on calmer seas to sail -
A steady job where I couldn't fail.
I later found, despite the welcome lull,
A civil servant's life is very dull.

Keith Collins

THE BOND

There's a bond that unites us here met tonight.
You can't see it, can't touch it,
But it's warm and it's tight.
'Tis pride in our Regiment and more, much more,
For 'twas cast, shaped, true-tempered
In the furnace of war.

Full fifty years we've kept this tryst
First, to honour our comrades, still much missed,
Who fell in battle and were laid gently to sleep
In alien fields, on mountainsides steep,
And, as our numbers diminish with each passing year,
We forget not old friends who are no longer here.

Our homages paid we then meet in good cheer
And now laugh at those days of danger and fear.
That we were often afraid we admit without shame
For we stifled our fears and fought on just the same.
No heroes were we, mainly ordinary blokes
With a war to be won ere we got home to our folks.

We're no longer young or nearly as spry
As when we fought in the ranks of Sixteen DLI
But as the evening goes on our years seem to withdraw;
We're young once again and back in our war:
Not reliving the horrors but rather the flankers
We'd craftily worked on our senior rankers.
(And the failures that earned us a week or two's jankers.)

We speak of old pals and the fun that we had;
Remember the good times, make joke of the bad.
With a smile we recall how we agreed with our chums
That all non-coms and officers had unmarried mums.
Then, as in battle most proved themselves good, steady lads,
We had to concede they just might have had dads.

In good-hearted banter, supping wine, whisky or beer
We reflect on those days of that far yesteryear.
Memories flood back of both pleasures and sorrows
When we lived for the day, pondered not on the morrows.
Long days of boredom, bloody clashes of arms,
Stand-to at first light and evening alarms.

We talk of the girls and the stories we'd told
To persuade those young ladies to be willing and bold.
(Don't think this exclusive to just rank and file
Young 'gentlemen', too, knew how to beguile).
'Immoral behaviour!' the righteous did cry,
But we were young then, full-blooded, knew that soon
we might die.

In the warmth of good fellowship time seems just to fly
And too soon comes the hour when we say - not 'Goodbye'.
'See you next year,' is our cry as we part;
Not trite, empty words but a wish from the heart.
(We know not the future but ever optimists we
Of the old Sixteenth Battalion, Durham Light Infantry!)

This bond hard-forged in fires strong
Of bullet, shell and mortar-bomb,
'Neath sun and rain, in cloying mud,
In dangers shared, our comrades' blood,
Unites us still, grows stronger yet,
A warm presence when any of us are met.
It's an intangible link, like a close family tie,
That binds us in this brotherhood of *Sixteen DLI.*

Ken Lovell

THE 1996 POACHER

The light of day has left the sky - the night is here at last,
the bats are winging overhead - their squeaky radar pinging fast!
The poacher climbs the fencing, set to keep the poachers out,
his senses tuned in to perfection, should any bailiffs be about.

The fly fishermen have long gone home - he knows where lie the trout,
it's as quiet as a graveyard - as his trade he goes about.
No torch the poacher carries - but he needs his nerves of steel,
as a frightened rat - runs across his foot - with one almighty squeal!

He is now beside the water - once again he looks about,
for any human shadow, before his tackle he gets out,
Then from beneath his knee-length coat, draws out his poacher's
rod and reel,
complete with hook tied to the line (lob worms), the fishes' meal!

The water's warm, the air is cool - ideal for trout to bite!
He mounts a lob worm on the hook, and casts into the night.
Immediately the line pulls taut, that trout was waiting there,
the reel it screams - as seven pounds of 'rainbow' takes the air.

Water flies in all directions, the noise enough to wake the dead!
The rod takes on a mighty curve, as the trout stands on its head.
It makes three runs of fifty yards, before it knows it's beat!
Then it's drawn into the poacher's net - that tasty rainbow treat!

Four more are taken in this way - in the silence of the night,
all stowed away, in a plastic bag - in a bush, off to his right.
A distant bell chimes (2am) - so home it has to be,
With twenty pounds of rainbow trout - and every one quite free!

But the excitement isn't over yet - two figures, stand against the sky,
Our poacher spots their hidden wheels - boy, those bailiffs are so sly!
Those crafty little devils - must have coasted down the road,
With vehicle lights extinguished - to catch the poacher with his load!

But a poacher has to stay ahead - or bag a hefty fine!
the penalty even heavier - should he be caught again, next time!
He has fished this spot so many times - he knows just what to do,
- and he melts into the forest dark and wet, with early morning dew.

The night is black as ink beneath the trees - he can barely see the sky,
No place for the faint-hearted, a night owl, hoots its screaming cry!
There are rustles in the bushes, enough to scare any mortal soul,
but he knows they are only animals, the foxes, rats and voles.

Those bailiffs they have now gone home - they never twigged that
he was there!
And being fully satisfied - they have vanished in thin air,
He left no tell-tale signs upon the bank, took everything away,
and for his cunning tidiness - ensures he can poach another day!

He now emerges from the wood - retrieves his hidden car.
Picks up his trout from where they lay - what a brilliant night, hoorah!
It isn't that he needs those trout - he enjoys his angling skill
For the hunter lurks in every man - I guess it always will!

It's just to be alone with nature - in the middle of the night!
To see the shooting stars go by - the herons in their flight,
But most of all, it's great to beat those bailiffs at their game!
(It's no good asking me to change - I shall always be the same!)

Edwin R Cracknell

SONNET: SPRING

I could not bear to walk with Wordsworth in the hills
And only view the crocus with despair
I'll use my feet to crush those daffodils
And close my mind to perfume in the air.
For you departed with melting winter's snow
Too delicate to cope with fractious life
And though I pleaded with you not to go
You slipped away from my despairing strife.
Let other gardens flourish from spring showers
I'll not look when roses fill my view
Shine sun on other people's flowers
And draw them from the earth that's taken you.

Then if as nectar the summer rain drips down
I'll raise my head and drink until I drown

E V Fox

OUR SKITTLE TEAM

'The Coronets' they call us
we play skittles for 'The Crown'
but no matter how we throw our balls
the pins just won't fall down
We thought a change of title
might help improve our game
but mine-host said that 'Big Boobs'
would give the pub a name
So come on girls let's practise more
'cause 'The Coronets' we stay
then we'll knock the living daylights
out of all pins in our way.

Mary Newman

INFORMATION

We hope you have enjoyed reading this book - and that you will continue to enjoy it in the coming years.

If you like reading and writing poetry drop us a line, or give us a call, and we'll send you a free information pack.

Write to :-

Anchor Books Information
1-2 Wainman Road
Woodston
Peterborough
PE2 7BU
(01733) 230761